Maybe
this will
explain why EC
is so weird. :i
Merry Christmas!
Elizabeth
-2008

On Solid Rock

THE FOUNDING VISION OF
FLORIDA PRESBYTERIAN / ECKERD COLLEGE

STEPHANIE KADEL TARAS, PH.D.

ISBN: 978-0-615-25573-6

Published by
Eckerd College
4200 54th Avenue South
St. Petersburg, Florida 33711
www.eckerd.edu

Cover art by
Robert Hodgell

Contents

Prologue

For a few weeks in the summer of 1962, Florida Presbyterian College had no faculty. All but two professors, plus the dean, submitted resignations to the board of trustees at the same time. These faculty members, some of the greatest minds and most talented teachers in the country, who had risked secure careers to come to this upstart institution, and who had worked countless hours in the past three years to create a college from scratch, were suddenly willing to let it go.

They were willing to let go of the innovative curriculum they had designed and fought over and nurtured day in and day out. They were willing to let go of their new home in the community of St. Petersburg, which had raised millions of dollars to bring the college to the sandy shores of Boca Ciega Bay. They were willing to let go of the best jobs of their careers, with excellent salaries, small classes, gifted colleagues, and plenty of room for experimentation.

And they were willing to let go of their students, the 150 founding freshmen who had joined them in taking a risk on a new institution, who had worked harder in their classes than they ever thought they could while creating a student culture for themselves, who would be juniors in the fall with two additional classes coming up behind them.

But through this drastic and painful act, the faculty were still teaching the students: teaching them about justice, about standing up for your beliefs, about holding leaders accountable, about what it means to be Christian.

That summer a black student had applied for admission to Florida Presbyterian College. He had graduated from St. Petersburg's all-black Gibbs Junior College, and there was no question among those who reviewed his application that he was qualified to transfer to Florida Presbyterian and join the class of 1964.

The all-white, mostly male faculty of FPC had come from both northern and southern states, but every one of them expected to be teaching in an integrated college. None of them would have come to Florida if he had thought the college would not accept black students. But the unthinkable happened: When the trustees heard about the new student, a slim majority voted not to accept him.

John Bevan, the dean of faculty, remembers, "I don't know of anything that has shaken me in higher education in my life experience more than that. It was the complete devaluation of everything we had done."

Bevan asked the president of FPC, William Kadel, what it would take to get the board back together and reconsider. Kadel said, "Resignations." By the next day, Bevan handed Kadel twenty-two resignations, with Bevan's own letter on top.

The deep passion the faculty felt for the vision of Florida Presbyterian College made it impossible to do otherwise. The college, as one early student remembered, was "not a place of what you should do, but of what you *must* do." The vision was of a learning community that tied together the life of the mind and the life of the spirit, that encouraged freedom with responsibility, that combined intellectual rigor with moral development. It offered students an interdisciplinary, holistic worldview and an opportunity to take risks.

But long before there were any students at Florida Presbyterian College, there were just a few men, carrying that vision like a lantern to light their way into an unknown and promising future.

CHAPTER 1

The Burning Bush

The administrative combination of an eloquent preacher-
president . . . who had no academic experience, and a
young, gifted teacher of psychology who had never been a
dean, proved to be the ideal team to lead us in the unique
and indescribably exciting work of creating a college.

Bill Wilbur[1]

The seawater that comes into Tampa Bay from the Gulf of
Mexico is calm. Waves do not crash the shore, and boaters rarely
worry about choppy conditions. In the mid-twentieth century
fish were still plentiful a short distance from any dock, so
northerners who had moved to Florida from various landlocked
states soon found themselves lured into the pleasurable, quiet
pastime of fishing.

This group included several men—professors and scholars—
who had come to Florida to help found a college. In the summer
of 1960 they were working seven days a week to prepare for
the arrival of the first class of students. But after spending the
previous winter in their former homes in less hospitable
climes, they had to make time for occasional beach trips and
fishing excursions.

Their leader, Jack Bevan, the dean of faculty who had hand-picked them for this job, was working harder than anyone else. One afternoon his faculty decided he needed a rest, so they offered to take Bevan fishing. Not a man who took his responsibilities lightly, Bevan reluctantly agreed. He tried to relax as the boat pulled away from the launch, but a life of ease was not in Bevan's repertoire. The whole time he was out on the boat, he gripped that fishing pole and shook it, saying, "Come on, fish! Get on there, fish!"

You could say Jack Bevan was a better fisher of men.

In 1959 no one had a stronger vision of what Florida Presbyterian College could become than Bevan. The board of trustees had a vision of a Presbyterian institution that would be good for the church and good for Florida. The president had a vision of a college that would do God's work for young people and the community. Jack Bevan, who was just thirty-three when he came to FPC as the first dean, had a vision for a great learning community that would push the boundaries of liberal arts education, offer students and faculty unprecedented freedom and support for intellectual pursuits, and continually challenge itself to explore what it means to be a Christian college.

Bevan had a charisma and charm that others seemed unable to resist. He is described as having a "booming" and "marvelous" speaking voice and able to deliver a speech off the cuff with "great aplomb." He had a commanding presence wherever he went. One of his faculty, John Satterfield, remembers, "He was a superbly convincing guy. He was just compelling in his talk."[2] During a faculty meeting about a change in the college calendar,

Bevan is reported to have once shouted, "I am not going to cram this down your throat!" while banging on the podium. Satterfield, who knew Bevan before FPC, when they were both professors at Davidson College in North Carolina, says Bevan had "untiring energy" and was always "wide awake in the morning and going until late at night."

Although not tall, Bevan could be imposing. He was stocky like a bear, with dark red hair that stood straight up and bushy eyebrows. "He mesmerized you with the eyebrows," says FPC athletic director Jim Harley. Students at FPC would come to nickname him "the burning bush."[3]

"He was so powerful and so incredibly intense," remembers founding freshman Carolyn Hall Horton. Carolyn took Bevan's psychology course in her junior year just so she could have him as a teacher. "He would always end statements with 'You see?' As if he was checking: 'You with me? You got it?'"

By all accounts Bevan had gotten it, and he wanted to bring everyone else along with him. "He was so dynamic, such a strong, forceful personality," says Katharine Meacham, the wife of founding faculty member Robert Meacham. "He had very high standards. And he was compassionate."

When Bevan went calling on men around the country, inviting them to teach at FPC, he made it impossible to say no. Not just because he was offering some of the highest salaries anywhere in the Southeast. Not just because he was offering the chance to create a college. Not just because he described a beautiful campus in a warm climate by the water. Bevan convinced men to leave tenured faculty positions, established programs, prestigious colleges, and longtime homes for a dream of a college like no other. He made them believe in the dream of Florida Presbyterian College because he believed in it with every cell of his fiery being.

John M. Bevan grew up in a Welsh, Methodist family just outside Wilkes-Barre, Pennsylvania. He was the second of four sons in a middle-class household; his father was a business manager in a feed and fertilizer store. Bevan graduated from Franklin and Marshall College in Lancaster and attended Evangelical and Reformed Theological Seminary in Lancaster for one year. He then moved to North Carolina, where he completed a bachelor of divinity degree at Duke University and met his wife, Louise. He went on to earn his master's and Ph.D. degrees in psychology at Duke, following in his older brother's footsteps, who was at Duke during the same years.

While attending classes full-time, Bevan also began preaching at two Methodist churches in the Durham area. Louise was impressed by her husband's ministering abilities. She remembers, "He was persuasive. He had a way of reaching people, of touching people."

Mid-way through his graduate education, Bevan taught two years at Heidelberg College in Tiffin, Ohio, before returning to Duke. Bevan had always wanted to be a teacher. "I guess, as I looked upon myself as to what contributed most to my own development," he says, "I always came up with the teachers I had had. . . . Teaching provided more of an answer to the solution of the world's problems, and a role anybody might play in that had the most to offer to young people."[4]

He always had a penchant for new and experimental ideas. At one point he was intrigued by parapsychology and worked in a Duke laboratory that was studying ESP. Bevan came to Davidson College to teach psychology to undergraduates in the early 1950s. By the late 1950s he and Louise had four children.

John Satterfield arrived at Davidson as a professor in the music department in 1953 and soon became good friends with Bevan. "He and I had some real reservations about Davidson College," says Satterfield, "and we had many talks. We helped start a discussion group among the faculty, which was unheard of then. We tried to read a book a month, and we got together and discussed it."

While at Davidson, Bevan got involved with the Faculty Christian Fellowship, a national organization with state chapters that held occasional weekend retreats to explore the role of a Christian teacher at the college level. Bevan joined a group of psychologists who were exploring this question, and he eventually served at the national level with the general committee, providing guidance for the work of the Fellowship. At that time Keith Irwin—who would join the FPC faculty as a professor of philosophy in 1961—was the Faculty Christian Fellowship's national coordinator, working out of an office in New York City. Irwin remembers Bevan as an "active organizer, but an academic in addition, somebody who had some sense of content, an exceptional person."

Also involved with education associations, Bevan was a "favorite" among members of groups like the American Association of Colleges. He would conduct workshops for them while learning about innovative ideas other colleges were trying. He heard about liberal arts colleges in the Northeast that were inviting the students to help develop the curriculum, replacing lectures with discussion groups, or experimenting with the academic calendar. He learned about an attempt by four New England colleges to create an experimental college that would have two semesters separated by an "interim term." During this one-month interim the campus would come together as an intellectual community and work on something together outside of separate classes. Even though this other college never quite got off the ground, Bevan did not forget these exciting new educational ideas.

"He was just a master at spotting trends in higher education as they were developing," says Satterfield. "When he came up with the curriculum for FPC, it was really astonishing, and it got all kinds of notice around the country very rapidly."

Bevan first heard about Florida Presbyterian College in 1958 from Hunter Blakely at a gathering of the Faculty Christian Fellowship in Montreat, North Carolina. Blakely, a national leader in the Presbyterian Church, is credited with originating the idea for a Presbyterian college in Florida.

Blakely must have been impressed, like so many others, with the young professor's enthusiasm, intelligence, and deep thinking about higher education. And he must have passed on that impression to FPC's founding president, William Kadel.

Bevan remembers, "When Bill Kadel contacted me to say he wanted to sit down and talk, the mere idea of planning a new institution was incredible. How many times would you have an opportunity like this? When else could you say: 'Let's start from scratch—what do you feel that students should get out of an education?'"

When, in January 1959, Kadel headed out on a tour of innovative college programs around the country, he asked Bevan to accompany him. Kadel was thinking about Bevan as the first dean of faculty, and this trip was a way to learn more about him and about how they would work together.

The trip was paid for by a grant from the Ford Foundation, and most of the ten institutions—including the University of Chicago; Miami University of Ohio; Penn State; Reed College in Portland, Oregon; Austin College in Sherman, Texas; and Occidental College in Los Angeles—had received Ford grants to encourage new ideas in higher education. The tour included a visit to the Ford Foundation's educational facilities research laboratory in New York.

When the trip was over, Bevan returned to teaching at Davidson, but he agreed to draft a suggested curriculum for the new Presbyterian college. The plan he designed valued interdisciplinary learning and disdained the traditional departmental divisions of most colleges and universities. Satterfield remembers that the departmental exclusivity at Davidson, which he and Bevan often lamented, seemed to suggest that there was "nobody responsible for—nobody, apparently, caring for—the integrity of the students' education." He saw Jack's plans for FPC as "a large step toward curricular responsibility."

This new curriculum included a four-year "Core program" of whole-group lectures and small-group discussions, to be taken by all students and taught by all faculty. In the freshman and sophomore years, the Core class would be called "Western Civilization and Its Christian Heritage."

The curriculum also emphasized independent study, reading and writing skills, foreign language study, and students taking responsibility for their own learning. It recognized faculty members as mutual learners along with their students and encouraged teaching methods that would help students experience the discovery of knowledge. It proposed what would come to be known as a 4-1-4 calendar, in which the month of

January would be set aside for intensive study of a single subject. This last element—later referred to as the interim term, winter term, January term, or midwinter semester— would turn out to be a hallmark of FPC's curriculum that would be quickly adopted by countless other colleges around the country.

After Bevan presented this innovative college program to the FPC trustees in February 1959, he considered his job over— until Bill Kadel called him a few weeks later and asked him to implement it.

Bevan remembers, "When suddenly, at the age of thirty-three, an opportunity like this came along, there was no way you could say no to it—there was no way."[5]

CHAPTER 2

Enter the Tigers

We simply didn't know what we couldn't do.

Billy Wireman

While Jack Bevan was completing his responsibilities at Davidson, he spent most of his time starting his job as dean of faculty for Florida Presbyterian College. One fact was painfully obvious: he did not have a faculty. Recruiting the best possible men as teachers, intellectuals, risk takers, and Christians was his top priority. The college made a commitment to pay much higher salaries than were common at the time to attract experienced, high-quality professors. The first year of classes, FPC was paying the fifth highest salaries in the South and the twenty-fifth highest in the nation.[6]

Bevan told Kadel and the board that FPC wanted "the kinds of individuals who teach in terms of a specialized discipline but are engaged with one another in a common discourse about values. . . . Of course, you want persons who have reputations as good teachers, people who have an interest in research and scholarship, so that it will be an ongoing process of the intellectual development of the campus. You want individuals who are responsive to students—that means, in a sense, their doors are open to students; they don't open the door for fifteen minutes a day, one day a week. . . . Humor is a factor that is always important, too, because in a situation where you're trying to build something, where there's going to be tension, you're going to have to have some humor."[7]

While he wanted a balance of liberals and conservatives, he also knew that this new institution could not be created by professors who wanted to preserve things the way they were in higher education. He wanted individuals who would be critical of ideas and examine them well enough to refine them. He inquired whether faculty were members of the American Association of University Professors (AAUP) because he felt that the support of that organization would be important to a new college, and he wanted to know what kind of commitment each individual had to his profession. He also sought teachers who cared about the student as a full person and wanted to see that person grow.

Bevan also had to consider religious affiliation. The college's charter required that faculty have "a belief in the fundamental teachings of Evangelical Christianity" (which meant, for example, no Jewish or Roman Catholic professors) and that two-thirds of the faculty be Presbyterian.[8] (These mandates were changed just a few years after the college opened to allow for faculty of all faiths.)

Bevan gathered names of potential faculty through several means. He called Keith Irwin at the Faculty Christian Fellowship and said, "I'm going to come to New York. I want to go through your membership list and find out who some of the best people are so I can get them on the faculty." He used his contacts in education associations and at the Danforth Foundation. (Danforth was a St. Louis–based foundation that was exploring the role of religion in higher education; faculty who became "Danforth Fellows" received small stipends to buy books on the topic and to entertain students in their homes to strengthen the faculty-student relationship). Bevan also turned to two of the colleagues he most respected at Davidson, John Satterfield and Pedro Trakas, and invited them to join him at FPC.

Eventually, he would also get to know contributors to *Motive* magazine, a highly regarded Methodist publication distributed to Christian colleges throughout the country. Although no founding faculty were involved with *Motive*, several later faculty found their way to FPC after contributing to the magazine, including visual artists Jim Crane, Peg Rigg, and Bob Hodgell; poet Peter Meinke; and philosopher Keith Irwin.

Most important, people came to Jack Bevan. As word got out about the new college and its innovative ideas, more than twelve hundred professors around the country eventually wrote to FPC, asking to be considered for one of the founding faculty positions.

"I think it would be right to say of Jack that he looked for rebelliousness and dissatisfaction with the conventional," says Satterfield, "but he wanted people who were really striving for the best. And he had time to find them." Unlike the typical faculty hiring process in which a search committee invites applicants to come to campus and be interviewed, Bevan traveled to most of his recruits' homes, observed them in the classroom, talked to their students, and met their families. By the time he got them down to St. Petersburg, Florida, the new home of FPC (where there was no campus yet to show off), he knew them well. And they were entranced by his vision.

"I remember Jack saying that his philosophy of starting the new school was to get a bunch of tigers and turn them loose," says founding faculty member Clark Bouwman.

Bevan would later say that during this recruiting process he felt "there was a hand guiding my hand."[9] He found men with deep roots in the church and expansive careers in liberal arts colleges, with tenured positions and the restless urge to start something new, with firsthand knowledge of war and the larger world and a commitment to peace and local action, with a clear sense of what was wrong with higher education and a willingness to take risks for something better. They were an impressive lot. But when they came to FPC, as Bevan's wife reflected, "they threw their prestige to the wind."

Albert Howard Carter II met Bevan and learned about FPC at an education conference, possibly the MLA (Modern Language Association). Carter came home and told his wife, "Jack Bevan is like my own brother. I love his whole idea to produce excellence." Bevan must have remembered Carter, too, because it was not long before he invited Carter to join other potential faculty at a curriculum planning meeting in St. Petersburg.

Forty-seven when he came to FPC, Carter was one of the most experienced professors of the group and was hired as chairman of the humanities division. A poet and an expert in comparative literature, he was known to be humorously eccentric, with a pipe always in his mouth to add to the dramatic effect. "He was a scream with his pipe," laughs his wife, Marjorie, many years later.

Raised in Chicago, Howard was the son of a doctor and a fiercely proud Scottish mother (whose favorite toast was "Here's to us who's like us"). Droll even as a little boy, he once came in from the backyard saying, "Here's a perfectly good dead squirrel."

In 1940 Howard married Marjorie, whom he had met at a professor's Christmas tea while he was a doctoral student at the University of Chicago. Marjorie came from a long line of professors ("I have, all my life, been in that cocoon," she says) and had studied at the Art Institute of Chicago and earned a master's degree in English. Her father insisted Howard have his Ph.D. before they married, so the ceremony took place two days after his oral exam. Howard always said, "I got a haircut, had my exam, and got married." The young couple moved during the war to Arlington, Virginia, where Howard worked on cryptanalysis for the Signal Corps. From there he became a professor in Fayetteville, Arkansas, where he was known for classroom antics, like singing a rendition of "St. Louis Blues" in French while wearing a straw hat.

Howard stayed at Fayetteville until the opportunity to help found Florida Presbyterian College grabbed him. He came to the planning meeting in December 1959, and he could hardly concentrate on his last semester of teaching in Arkansas. "The minute school was out, he dumped us all in the car," Marjorie remembers. "We were the first family to get here."

Like most of the founding faculty of Florida Presbyterian, Howard left a tenured university position to take a risk on this new college. He and Marjorie showed up in St. Pete with two teenage children (their son would be a founding freshman) and a dog. They lived for a short while in a dorm room on the temporary campus while they looked for a house. St. Pete "was a little dopey to us," she remembers, "not as peppy as Chicago," but as more faculty and their families arrived, the Carters and their new friends found ways to enjoy their new surroundings— during the rare hours when they were not working.

"He was an idealist," says Marjorie, "and here he came to enact his dreams." Carter thought every person should go to a great college, and he often espoused that farmers should take classes and read poetry during the winter months. Very bright and deeply religious, he saw learning as a path to God's purpose for one's life; students "could look into life and see all the deeper meanings and they could be made happy by a vision," explains his wife. "He felt obligated as a Christian to do a great deal of the things he did."

Bevan remembers that Carter thought nothing was impossible. Any idea was worth trying—now or tomorrow, but certainly not next week. During FPC's first winter term in January 1961, the dean of students came to Bevan and said, "We're missing six female students. I don't know whether they did or did not return. Nobody seems to know where they are."

Bevan asked, "Who are they working with?"

"They're all working under Howard Carter."

"Well, then," said Bevan, "your answer is as good as mine."

They went to Carter and asked if he knew where the students were. Carter rubbed his nose and said, "One may be at the University of Chicago Library, one may be at the University of North Carolina at Chapel Hill, one at the Folger Library. I'm not sure, but they're all out there, and they're supposed to be back at the end of the month."

The dean wondered what the college should tell the parents if they called. And Carter said, "They're just out learning, and it's a big world out there, and they're at the right place. That's all I can say."[10]

When a student in Carter's discussion group for Western Civilization complained that Carter's grading system seemed very subjective, Carter said, while puffing on his pipe, "Young man, it's my opinion of your work that they pay me for." He once suggested in a faculty meeting that they give students green stamps instead of grades.

Carter stayed at FPC for the rest of his career, which ended all too soon, in 1970, when he died from cancer of the brain. Jim Harley, the longtime athletic director at the college, remembers being told a story about Carter's last days by a student named David Glass (who graduated in 1971). When Glass went to see Harley one summer day, Harley asked him what he was up to.

"Well, I'm driving a garbage truck for the City of St. Petersburg," said David. "And another thing I've been doing is I've been going over to see Dr. Howard Carter. I read to him. When I went in the other day, I said, 'How are you, Dr. Carter?' And he didn't open his eyes. So I said, 'I've got the dirtiest job in the world this summer. What do you think that is?' And without moving his eyes or anything, he just said, 'Registrar.'"

John Satterfield was happy to leave Davidson at Bevan's invitation and become FPC's first associate professor of music. Satterfield, thirty-nine, was still finishing his Ph.D. degree at the University of North Carolina at Chapel Hill (UNC), but he was already known for his original jazz compositions and big band arrangements. He came to Florida with his wife, Carolyn, and four children, one of whom was mentally handicapped and difficult to manage.

Born and raised in Danville, Virginia, Satterfield was the first in his family to graduate from college. Satterfield's father, a Purple Heart recipient in the Great War, shoveled coal for the railroad before he became an engineer on a diesel train. He was also chairman of the local railroad union. Satterfield admired his father's "quality of being so much himself and devoted to his profession."

Satterfield's precociousness landed him in third grade at the age of six and out of high school by sixteen. He began studying the piano at ten, when, he remembers, "I ran into a jazz player who was about six years older than I was, and that ruined my professional career as a legitimate pianist." He majored in trumpet at UNC but let little get in the way of jazz piano. "I slept until afternoon, hardly ever went to a class, stayed up all night playing music. When the music building was locked, I broke into the Methodist church, and played until four or five o'clock in the morning and went home and went to sleep."

Satterfield recalls one professor in a philosophy course who claimed that "if it can't be said in words, it can't be said, and if it can't be said, it doesn't have meaning." Says Satterfield, "Well, that was the end of that class for me." The chairman of the music department tagged him as "bright but extremely rebellious." Satterfield once told him, "I'd rather write one page of decent music than a whole library full of prose about music."

Just when he might have flunked out of school, Satterfield was drafted into the army air corps and went to war. He served in Europe as a communications officer, essentially keeping the radios working in planes. When he got back to UNC, wiser and anxious for credentials to "amount to something," he had no more trouble in school. He went on for a master's degree in music, arranging Cole Porter and Duke Ellington tunes for an eighteen-piece big band on the weekend, while writing a suite for orchestra for his thesis that won him a composer's prize.

As Satterfield's musicianship developed, so did his theories about education. When an English professor said, "Just think, my dear students, what criticism has done for Shakespeare," Satterfield thought, "How can any statement be more absurd? And for somebody to say, 'Oh, he is a renowned Dante scholar' used to burn me up. Why isn't he a renowned Dante?"

With a wife and child in 1949, Satterfield took a job teaching music in the South Carolina public schools. He traveled between an elementary, middle, and high school. Compared to the extraordinary musical opportunities presented by the GI-infused bands of UNC, working with untrained and unruly children was a huge disappointment. "I used to get up every morning and vomit," he remembers. Soon, however, he got a position at Davidson College and began work on his doctorate.

Satterfield left Davidson after seven years to come to Florida. Why did Bevan ask his treasured colleague to join him in this venture? Says Satterfield, "I can just joke and say he had a bad dream or something. But he said that he wanted the best people he could get down there, and I was very honored he chose Pedro Trakas and me."

During his years at FPC Satterfield would come to be known for a legendary Western Civilization lecture titled "Myth and Symbol" in which he played piano, used props and live animals on stage, and joked about his faculty colleagues. All the while, he was using a circular presentation of questions and stories to explore definitions of myth, symbol, analogy, and allegory through the fields of religion, philosophy, psychology, science, history, art, poetry, and music, and he tied it together with references to *Moby-Dick* (the required reading for the week in which he gave the lecture). The entertaining talk was so popular that students would come back year after year to hear it. But they would still say they never really figured out what it was about.

Grover Wrenn, a founding freshman, remembers writing a paper for Satterfield on T. S. Eliot. Now, at sixty-two years old, Grover still remembers what Satterfield wrote on the paper: "Mr. Wrenn, your writing is technically precise, if uninspired."

Early in Satterfield's time at FPC, two colleagues would volunteer to teach his courses one term so he could finish his dissertation and earn his Ph.D. degree. "What a generous, loving bunch of people," he says of his fellow faculty members.

One Sunday morning in the fall of 1958, William C. Wilbur read a notice in the *New York Times* headlined "Church Selects Site for College." The article described a new Presbyterian college that had just found its home in St. Petersburg, Florida. "It sounded kind of exciting," Wilbur remembers, "and I was at the point where I was getting fed up with my boss."

Wilbur was forty-three and well into a career as a tenured history professor at Muhlenberg College in Allentown, Pennsylvania. A small, soft-spoken man, he was a committed teacher but had become somewhat disillusioned by administrative decisions there. He was also sick of shoveling snow. So he took a chance and wrote a letter.

"Then, lo and behold, Jack turned up in Allentown in the spring. He called me and said that he was in the area and he'd like to come by and talk to me." Bevan specifically wanted to come to Wilbur's home. His wife, Pat, was "horrified at the short notice." Before Bevan left that day, Wilbur had been invited to a curriculum planning session in St. Pete.

Wilbur was hooked. "Jack was so enthusiastic about what was going to happen at this place. It was such an intriguing idea to create it from scratch. No rules, and the faculty would have a great role in deciding what kind of a place it might be. It was exciting, and you couldn't believe, really, it was going to be quite as good as it turned out to be." When he was offered a faculty position, Wilbur did not hesitate. He left his tenured position and moved his family to Florida. It may have been one of the biggest chances he ever took.

Bill's father was in the real estate and insurance businesses in Charleston, South Carolina, and an active member of the Southern Baptist church. He was able to afford to send his children to college, even during the Depression, and Bill attended Washington and Lee University in Lexington, Virginia. "In my senior year, they raised the tuition to $275," Wilbur remembers. "Everybody thought that was outrageous."

Bill's mother, the daughter of a Georgia doctor, helped Bill with his French classes. And Bill's paternal grandmother encouraged his love of history by telling him stories of the Civil War and of meeting Mrs. Robert E. Lee.

Wilbur remembers the "close contact of student and faculty" when he was a student and the history professors who inspired him. "History deals with people and personalities and what happened in the past which influences how we are in the present, and I was always fascinated with that," he says. "And I had grown up in Charleston, which is sort of living history." Wilbur went on to graduate school at Columbia University in New York to study British history.

But when the war started in England, he had to put his research on hold, which is when he first started teaching at Muhlenberg. Then, in 1942, he was drafted into the army, where he served primarily as a cryptographic officer and also kept records of his squadron's activities ("I was the squadron historian,

19

so to speak"). In looking back on his war experience, Bill says, "The thing that struck me most was seeing the destruction and realizing how fragile civilization really is."

Bill met his wife, Martha, known to everyone as "Pat," during the war. She was born in China, the daughter of a missionary. When Bill (a Southern Baptist) and Pat (a Methodist) married in 1946 and moved back to Allentown, they decided to join the First Presbyterian Church. Bill finished his dissertation research and completed his doctorate in the early 1950s. He continued teaching at Muhlenberg for another fourteen years until he came to FPC.

Wilbur was less flamboyant than some of the other faculty and more likely to argue for tried-and-true educational practices. Bevan would later remember Wilbur as "the chap who always examined the question and always had one more question to ask. Things were perfected as a result of him."[11]

When Robert Meacham was invited to St. Petersburg to help plan the curriculum for FPC, he was already in Florida as a tenured professor teaching mathematics to graduate students at the University of Florida in Gainesville. He thought he had no interest in working with freshmen again. But Bevan, who probably got Meacham's name from the Faculty Christian Fellowship, wanted the accomplished mathematician and teacher on his team. He went to Gainesville to try to convince Meacham.

"Come plan the math curriculum," said Bevan. "You don't have to promise."

"Okay," said Meacham. "But I'm just telling you the truth. I'm not interested."

When Meacham got to the planning meeting, he called his wife, Katharine, and said, "This is the most exciting thing I have ever encountered. I want you to come meet these people."

Katharine answered, "I love Gainesville. I'm never leaving." Six months later they had moved to St. Pete.

It had been a long journey for Bob Meacham to this point. The fifth of six children in Birmingham, Alabama, Bob was the son of a Presbyterian minister, but his father was ill during the Depression, and the family struggled. Bob got a scholarship to Southwestern College (now Rhodes) in Memphis, to which he hitchhiked from home. He waited tables in the college dining room, became president of the honor council, tutored other students, and began to distinguish himself as a leader. He looked like a leader, standing over six feet tall with polished good looks and what his daughter would later call "that million-watt smile."

Katharine Miller must have noticed him in an economics class in 1940, when she was a sophomore and he was a junior. Katharine was a member of a prominent Memphis family. Her father was a doctor and administrator at University of Tennessee Medical College. Her mother was a 1906 graduate of Vanderbilt and an adjunct professor. Her grandfather was a Presbyterian minister. Bob noticed Katharine in class and asked her for a date.

After graduating, they married just before the navy sent him to the Pacific as a submarine officer of radar during World War II. Katharine went to Radcliffe (Harvard's program for women) to study business administration. After the war Bob went to Brown University for his graduate degrees in applied mathematics.

While still a student at Southwestern, Meacham had done a little teaching and discovered he liked it and was good at it. "Teaching was the only thing he'd ever considered," says

Katharine. After five years as a professor at Carnegie Institute of Technology (now Carnegie Mellon) in Pittsburgh, they moved to Gainesville with three of their eventual four children. During the summers Meacham worked at Cape Canaveral, where he wrote the mathematical equation for rockets in flight.

Meacham was forty when he came to FPC. He stayed the rest of his life. The hall clock in his family's house was set ten minutes early because that's how long it took to drive to the college. "The College," his younger daughter, Laura, remembers. "No other identification was needed."

"He never, ever, hesitated to stick his nose into anything he felt needed his involvement," says Laura. "Crises arrived like clockwork, but Daddy loved it. Always, after careful discussions with my mother, he would produce 'A Letter.' This letter would outline his analysis of the situation and his proposals for resolution."

The Meachams joined Lakeview Presbyterian Church in central St. Pete, and Bob's weekly routine included driving his Volkswagen camper onto the FPC campus to pick up students for church and for Sunday dinner at his home afterward.

His children would eventually grow up to attend FPC/Eckerd. They would take his math classes. His son, Robert, almost failed. When Professor Meacham told him his midterm grade was an F, Robert's response was, "I hope my parents don't find out!"

Says daughter Laura, "I still cannot set foot on this campus without a swell of pride that my father gave his professional life so that this college could emerge from dreams to reality."[12]

Clark Bouwman did not wait for Bevan to come to him. He was visiting his parents (who had retired to Florida) in 1958, when his father told him about a new college in St. Pete. Jack Bevan had not even been hired yet. But Bouwman arranged a meeting with the president, Bill Kadel, and they ended up talking for a couple of hours about plans for the college and Clark's teaching experience and interests. He was then invited down to the planning meetings in September and December 1959 and hired onto the faculty after that.

Bouwman, who was hired as associate professor of sociology, was forty-one in 1960. He had completed his master's and doctorate at the New School for Social Research in New York and had taught sociology at Western Michigan University and at Upsala College in East Orange, New Jersey. He left a position as head of the Department of Sociology at Illinois Wesleyan University when he came to FPC.

Bouwman was born in Grand Rapids, Michigan, but moved around the Midwest during his childhood. His father was a Northern Baptist minister and lifelong socialist who raised his son to believe "that society can continue to evolve and perfect itself if we follow Jesus' teachings, and that evolvement will move in the direction of more and more social cooperative effort." Bouwman's parents expected him to go to college, and he graduated from Kalamazoo College in 1941, just before he joined the Merchant Marines.

About World War II, Bouwman says, "I was in the strange situation of feeling this was a war that needed to be fought and won against Hitler, but I also was a pacifist and not wanting to be in the position of presumably killing somebody." Curiously, he was stationed for some time at the maritime base in St. Petersburg that would eventually be FPC's first campus.

He married his wife, Pat, in 1943, and she came to St. Pete for a year to live with him.

After the war Bouwman got a second bachelor's degree in social sciences at Western Michigan and attended Yale Divinity School for a year, but he needed to start earning a living for his family. So, when Western Michigan called to ask him to teach sociology, they moved back west. During that first year of college teaching, Bouwman "decided it was so great that that was what I would make my life career." At Upsala College, a Lutheran school, he found he preferred "a church-related, small liberal arts college where personal relationships were an important factor. . . . It was the teacher-student relationship that meant the most to me."

That's what he talked about with Kadel in 1958. And it was no doubt a primary emphasis of those planning meetings with his new FPC colleagues, whom he remembers all shared the excitement of starting a new school. "There was just something phenomenal about the responsibility and joy of seeing what we talked through theoretically become actual practice with students," Bouwman remembers.

Years later Bevan would call Bouwman a "one-man international force." He planned the first study abroad program for FPC students, taking a January term class to Mexico to study the culture and language. It was one of many trips he would organize for students and faculty colleagues. He left the classroom after a few years to head up international study programs for the college, which included negotiating the long-term lease for the "London Study Centre." Over subsequent years in administrative roles, Bouwman would serve as dean of students, dean of admissions, and dean of special programs, through which he helped to create the Program for Experienced

Learners (PEL)—a degree-granting program of evening classes for older, nonresidential students; the English Language Study program; and the first Elderhostel program outside of New England.

Billy Wireman says he "encountered" Bill Kadel and Jack Bevan when he was only twenty-six years old and just out of graduate school. "They could do a number on you," he remembers. "They laid out the vision of the college, and I'll never forget it—I've quoted it a thousand times—'To capture the imagination not only of Florida but of the American public as well.'"

Wireman had heard about the college from his wife, Katie, who heard about it from her friend Shirley West. Shirley was married to Tom West, who had recently been hired as FPC's first director of admissions (see Chapter Five). West apparently told Bevan to look into Wireman for the position of associate director of physical education. Before he knew it, Wireman was in Florida at an interview. He remembers, "Dr. Kadel as a connection to the church and a great speaker and inspirational figure, highly respected in the church, and Jack Bevan who was a towering intellect from Davidson—that combination of those two gentlemen, when you met with them the first time, you were just overwhelmed with opportunity, promise, a sense of excitement."

Wireman was looking for a job. He had just finished a year of teaching at Shepherd College in West Virginia, during which time he had nearly completed his doctorate in education and inferential statistics from Peabody College (now part of Vanderbilt University) in Nashville. In 1957-58, just before going back to school, he had been an assistant basketball coach under the famed Adolph Rupp at the University of Kentucky. The team won the national championship that year. Wireman was on his way to "big-time coaching." But he had a restlessness about him, an undefined desire to do more.

As an only child growing up in Kentucky, Billy felt "loved beyond measure." His family was comfortably well-off, thanks to a generous settlement from the government when Billy's grandfather was killed in the First World War. They were devout Presbyterians. His father, who had two years of college, worked as a supervisor in an ammunitions facility in Fort Knox. He also liked to cook. In fact, after Billy left for college, his parents opened a restaurant. Billy never forgot the taste of his father's fried green tomatoes.

"He was a big sports fan," Billy remembers of his dad. They went to a lot of college games together, and Billy played football, basketball, and baseball in high school. He was an average student with a particular interest in history. He expected to go to college on an athletics scholarship.

One morning Billy was waiting outside his house, with a packed bag, for a bus to take him to Morehead State College in Morehead, Kentucky, to begin his freshman year. He was not crazy about it, however, because Morehead told him he could only play football there. Billy had wanted to go to Georgetown College, but they had not called. As he waited for the bus, it started to rain, and he went back inside his house. The phone rang, and it was Georgetown calling, saying he was accepted and could play all three sports there if he wanted.

Wireman was an undersized athlete but an obvious leader. He remembers his interview with Rupp when he was twenty-four and "scared to death."

Rupp asked him, "Can you recruit for me the best basketball players in the world?"

Wireman said, "Coach Rupp, I'll try."

And Rupp said, "Goddammit boy, the last guy tried. That's the reason he ain't here." It was a good lesson for Billy.

When he came to FPC, he did more than try. He created a studious approach to physical education, with seminars on the history of sport, the role of recreation in society, and the value of physical activity in relieving stress and fostering creativity. He taught students how to sail, and he recruited German professor Ken Keeton to coach a tennis team. He pulled together a respectable basketball team in a program that had no athletic scholarships, no gym, and a handful of talented young players who had come to college primarily to get an education, not to play sports.

Wireman also turned out to be a gifted development officer. Kadel began taking him on calls to potential donors and to dinners and events. Wireman was a man who could communicate the vision of Florida Presbyterian College and, indeed, capture the imagination of the public. He was destined for much more than a coaching job. FPC just didn't know it yet.

Perhaps Bevan's colleague at Davidson, Pedro Trakas (who would be FPC's first Spanish teacher), provided the name of Kenneth Keeton as a potential professor of German. Keeton and Trakas already knew each other from language teacher conferences. However it happened, one day Bevan found his way to Salem, North Carolina, where Keeton was teaching at Wake Forest. Keeton met Bevan at his hotel and didn't leave until two in the morning. "We talked and talked, and I thought, 'What a remarkable human being.' And when he laid out the program for the college, I said, 'This is Utopia!'"

Bevan described a plan to require three years of foreign language study for all students—a policy guaranteed to fill Keeton's classes and enable students to learn to speak German or Spanish or French more fully than they could with just a couple of semesters. Keeton also learned that the new college would build a state-of-the-art language lab, encourage international travel and study, and allow student exchange across countries. These were just the kinds of learning opportunities Keeton had been fighting for at Wake Forest, but, he remembers, "in a very conservative school, everything was so hard to accomplish." Keeton, who was thirty-two when Bevan came calling, was also interested in helping students outside the classroom and was pleased to learn that Bevan sought teachers who cared about the whole student.

At the end of the meeting, says Keeton, "I clapped my hands. I thought, 'Boy, that's it for me.' I didn't even ask my wife. I went home and said, 'We're moving.'" He never even asked about salary. "It never interested me at all. I was just so excited about the program." He was later pleased to discover it was double his Wake Forest salary.

The last child of a poor carpenter in rural western Kentucky, Keeton had always kept an eye out for opportunities to work and to learn. He was active in the local Baptist church where he found work as a janitor, playground director, and choir director. He also got a job as a soda jerk in a drugstore, and he rode his bike six miles to work on a farm for a dollar a day. He studied French and Spanish in school and sang in the choir. He was athletic and quick, with a dimpled smile and twinkling eyes.

In 1945 Keeton was drafted into the army at eighteen. Although the war was just about over, he served a year as a courier with the occupational forces in Germany. He learned the German language, saw much of the country, and fell in love with German opera. At nineteen, he was discharged and came back to Kentucky. With the GI Bill he decided to go to college like his older sister, who had been the first in his family to do so. At Georgetown in Kentucky he majored in German and minored in Spanish. He did well in the classes he liked and poorly in the classes he didn't. He went on for a master's degree at the University of Kentucky and then took his wife and new baby to Wake Forest, where he taught German and Spanish.

He found he "had a knack for teaching" but realized he didn't know enough about German literature to do the job he wanted to do. So Keeton began work during the summers on a doctorate at the University of North Carolina. He finished his degree in 1956 and taught four more years at Wake Forest. During that time he helped students create a pub for dancing in an old stable adjacent to the campus (because dancing was banned by the Baptist college). He also tried to bring an African student to Wake Forest (who would have been the first black student there), but it was not approved. He was able, however, to create the first study abroad program, taking students to Germany in the summer of 1960, which delayed his arrival at FPC until just a week before the students showed up.

Bevan's recruiting of founding faculty for Florida Presbyterian College was complete with nineteen professors (see Appendix A) and a few additional instructors and assistants.

Sixty-eight percent were Presbyterians, and seven other evangelical denominations were represented in the remaining 32 percent. Their average age was thirty-seven.

Pedro Trakas came as a professor of Spanish from Davidson. He had earned his Ph.D. degree at Harvard and was fluent in Spanish, Greek, Italian, French, and Latin. He was also an expert on the use of language laboratories (using recording equipment to help students study language lessons). Satterfield remembers Trakas as "recognized all over the Davidson campus as far and away the single best classroom performer in language teaching there."[13]

Jim Harley remembers Trakas as "the greatest teacher, because I could stop there at midnight, and he'd be getting ready for tomorrow's class. He was an experienced teacher, but he didn't want anybody to think he hadn't prepared."

Bevan found physicist I. G. "Iggy" Foster at Virginia Military Institute and brought him down to chair the math and sciences division. Foster believed so passionately in this new college that later he would be one of only two faculty who refused to resign over the board's failure to accept the school's first black student. Foster would teach at the college until his death almost forty years later.

John Dixon, an art historian from Dickinson College, "could point a hard finger at the rest of us and what we were doing at times," Bevan remembers.[14] Others tell stories that suggest Dixon had little sense of humor and was therefore often the butt of colleagues' jokes. He only stayed at FPC a few years.

Dexter Squibb, a chemistry professor, saw several familiar faces among the founding freshman class. He had created a summer science program for exceptional high school students when he taught at Western Carolina College. A few of those students, including Grover Wrenn (see Chapter Five), decided to follow him to Florida Presbyterian College.

George Reid came from Rutgers University to be a professor of biology. A later biology professor, John Ferguson, remembers Reid's "dedication and self-sacrifice" on the college's behalf a few years after the founding: "It was, I believe, 1968, and George Reid, senior professor in biology had just completed a several-year-long hard effort in writing a new textbook for general biology (*Bioscience*—a fine book that was well received). However, the then two very young members of the discipline, Bill Roess and myself, were brimming with innovative ideas for alternative ways of teaching biology. Reid responded warmly to our suggestions, and the discipline quickly revised its course offerings into a Core-type experience emphasizing the progressive development of skills. In this new curriculum general biology, as a separate course, was no longer offered. Thus, George Reid never got to use his textbook in his own course, and he never expressed hesitation or regret at the turn in direction. The new curriculum went on to become highly successful."[15] Reid would also be an early spokesman for environmental conservation, even though his knowledge and views would fall on deaf ears in the initial physical development of the campus.

E. Ashby Johnson, a professor of religion and philosophy from Austin College in Sherman, Texas, had such a heavy southern accent that he made the other southerners on the faculty sound positively northern. "Ashby enjoyed being a southern gentleman," Bouwman remembers, "but, at the same time, he was very liberal and progressive in everything."

Bill Wilbur recounts a story of Johnson talking to a woman about where she was going to send her son to college. She didn't want him to go to one of *those* colleges where they have all kinds of funny, radical ideas, so she was thinking he might go to Presbyterian College in South Carolina, which was Johnson's alma mater. Johnson said to the mother, "Well you're perfectly safe, Mrs. So-and-So. He won't get any ideas there at all."

At Austin College Johnson (who had a doctorate of theology from Union Theological Seminary) had directed an experimental program in interdisciplinary education, which Kadel and Bevan visited during their tour of colleges. He remembers, "I was tickled pink when I was invited to come to St. Petersburg over the Christmas holidays of 1959 to talk about the new college. I did not have a firm offer of a position, but the implication was that I was being considered for the staff. . . . There was no question in my mind that if I could get in on the deal, *I would be there!* I didn't try to fool myself or anybody else on that. If I could, I was going to get in on it."[16] He says he was ready to quit asking, "How do you revise and revamp a curriculum?" and instead ask, "How do you provide a first-rate education in the middle of the twentieth century?" Johnson was hired to direct FPC's Western Civilization program.

At FPC Johnson would often join Satterfield, Carter, Wilbur, and classics professor Fred White (who came from Beloit College and was fifty when he arrived at FPC) in a regular game of wit. "It was a kind of intellectual dueling," Bevan remembers, "an exercise of intellect." Others might try to participate but would quickly find themselves over their heads. "But everyone would be laughing by the end."[17] When White was on vacation one summer, he apparently drove two hundred miles out of his way to mail a letter to Ashby Johnson from Sherman, Texas, where Johnson had lived. All it said was, "War was right. Sherman is hell." Satterfield remembers White as "the most masterful prepared lecturer I have ever heard."

Other founding faculty included Dennis Anderson, an instructor in biology from Iowa State University; Guy Owen Baker, a music professor who came from Tulane University to direct FPC's first choir; Everett Emerson, an English professor from Lehigh University; Robert Hall, a French instructor from Chapel Hill; and Jack Wilson, a math professor from Central College, Iowa. The first chaplain at FPC was professor of religion Alan Carlsten, who came in 1961, replacing Creighton Peden, a theology student from Chicago who served as chaplain assistant in the college's first year.

The only women involved in the first year's teaching were Bettye Rae Crane (instructor in physical education), Florence Sherbourne (assistant professor in developmental English and reading), and Frances Whitaker (dean of women). While women were not unheard of as professors in higher education in the late 1950s, they were not prominent in prestigious colleges and universities like the ones Bevan was visiting. Satterfield remembers that the first woman professor was not hired at Davidson until after he left, and the decision caused "grumbling." He adds, "I can't say that was heavily on my mind in 1960."

Despite his progressive thinking about higher education, the value of women on the faculty was apparently not much on Bevan's mind either, nor was the value of faculty of color. While he was certainly aware of and supportive of the civil rights movement, the time of attention to diversity in the classroom had simply not yet arrived.

But when his faculty arrived in St. Petersburg in 1960, they discovered that Bevan's dream for a college of distinction was well on its way toward reality. Several years of work had already gone into the development of Florida Presbyterian College before they had even heard of it.

CHAPTER 3

God's Dreamer

It would never occur to me that the college could have come into existence without God's help. God's help was exerted through all of us . . . in a positive, meaningful, loving kind of way.

Clark Bouwman

In 1955 the First Presbyterian Church of Orlando was fast becoming the largest Presbyterian church in the state of Florida. The church's members numbered two thousand in 1953 and would grow to almost four thousand by 1958. They worshipped in a stately building, with six large columns creating an imposing façade, topped by a steeple that lofted a cross high above the neighborhood.

They came to hear Bill Kadel preach. When he stepped up to the pulpit—a man of average height, a bit pudgy, with graying hair and black-rimmed glasses, dressed in a long black robe—he would smile at the congregation, his eyes would sparkle, and everyone knew he had a story to tell. Kadel always had a good story that led to a good message and that made his listeners want to be good people. He didn't threaten fire and brimstone. He believed in the beneficence of God, and he wanted to help everyone find the comfort of a closer walk with God in daily life.

He even started a daily "dial-a-prayer" service that offered a recorded prayer in Kadel's voice to over 750 callers from throughout Orlando each day.

"I remember him as being so warm. He made you feel like you were really important," says Carolyn Hall Horton, who grew up in the Orlando church and eventually became a founding student at FPC. She describes Kadel as "very much a spiritual leader" who was highly respected at his church. But she also had the impression that "people used to talk out of the sides of their mouths that he was a dreamer" with his plans for the future. "People would wonder how he was going to make all these things happen."

Kadel proved he was not as naïve as folks had feared. Within eighteen months of his arrival Kadel and the church members had raised $300,000 to complete the fund-raising for a new sanctuary. A year after it was built, they raised almost $600,000 more for a new educational building. Kadel's efforts also smoothed tensions between factions within the church, creating a welcoming environment for all the new members.

"Perhaps I have been successful in challenging people to give of their substance to God," Kadel said in 1958. "I presented Christianity as a compelling religion which demands their best, their talent and their love."[18]

One morning in 1955 Kadel was not preaching or fund-raising or overseeing plans for new church buildings. He was taking a moment to dream, along with others. He was participating in a meeting, held at his church, in which Presbyterian leaders and laypeople from around the state were discussing the possibility of a church-related college in Florida.

It was Hunter Blakely's idea originally. Former president of Queens College in Charlotte, North Carolina, Blakely was secretary of the Division of Higher Education of the Board of Education of the Presbyterian Church, U.S., from 1950 to 1962. From his office in Richmond, Virginia, Blakely had been paying attention to Florida's phenomenal population growth (projected to be over six million by 1970) and the expectation that the college-age population in the state would increase 99 percent in fifteen years. He also noted that Presbyterian church membership was on the rise in Florida; from 1940–50, church membership had increased by 70 percent, while the population rose by just 46 percent. He knew that Presbyterians were experienced at starting colleges: by the Civil War they had started forty-nine colleges and universities in twenty-one (of the then thirty-four) states. Florida was the only state in the nation without a Presbyterian college.[19]

Blakely got the Presbyterian Church, U.S. (which had split from the larger Presbyterian Church, U.S.A., in 1861, and became known as the "Southern" church) to designate 1954 as the year for emphasis on higher education. During that time he discussed his idea for a Florida college with a small group of clergy, including Kadel.

These talks led to a forty-member council of representative Presbyterians, charged by the Synod of Florida (the state leadership of the church) to explore the idea. And now here they were, in Kadel's church, electing a layperson as chairman of the council and a clergyman as vice chairman. Philip J. Lee, vice president of the Atlantic Coast Line Railroad, was elected chairman. Kadel was called away from the meeting to the telephone when the group elected him vice chairman.

Kadel remembers Lee was too busy to do a lot of the "spade work," so Kadel spent a lot of time traveling the state, visiting churches, and talking to laypeople about the "character of the institution" the church wanted to create.[20] Through these meetings a volunteer board of trustees for the college was formed, and fund-raising began.

At the same time, Blakely requested a feasibility study, paid for by the church's Board of Education, to be conducted by Gordon W. Blackwell, director of the Institute for Research in Social Science at Chapel Hill, and Francis Rosecrance, Associate Dean of Education at New York University. In an October 1956 report they concluded that a liberal arts college should be established in Florida but that it would need to be of outstanding quality, with a high degree of creativity and vision, to succeed at a state and national level.

Kadel remembers that the initiators of the FPC concept felt there was no place in America for just another college. If it was worth doing at all, it was worth going first-class, committing to "top-flight faculty," an innovative curriculum, selectivity in admissions to ensure "superior students," and facilities that would foster this quality.[21] They believed it would be easier to raise funds for a quality institution. And they were explicit about this emphasis. The first promotional handbook about the college, published to recruit students, states that, "Certain kinds of curriculum and methods of teaching are possible and appropriate only with superior students. Excellent opportunities now exist for college education for average and below-average students, but outstanding students have only limited opportunities."[22]

With the feasibility study in hand, the Florida Synod voted in May 1958 to establish "Florida Presbyterian College" and approved the college's charter and slate of trustees. It would be the first Presbyterian college established in the United States in sixty-five years. On May 27 the board of trustees met for the first time and elected Philip Lee as the first chairman of the board and Bill Kadel as the college's president. Bill's wife, Kay, remembers, "We were up in Pennsylvania on vacation when Bill got a call that he had been made president of this new college that wasn't yet."

Starting a college from scratch might have felt like a daunting task to Kadel and Lee, but in the 1950s anything seemed possible. It was a time of buoyant optimism in the United States. After winning the Second World War, the nation was taking its place as a world leader. Leaving behind a time of rationing, the country needed several years to catch up on car manufacturing and house building, but by the 1950s—after refitting ammunitions factories into manufacturing facilities for home appliances—middle-class households and new suburban homes were being filled with luxury consumer goods. Veterans who went to college on the GI Bill, many the first generation in their families to do so, had greater opportunities for jobs to support their wives and baby boom children. The success of the war suggested to them that any problem could be solved with resources, ingenuity, and enough hard work.

At the same time, this newfound prosperity had to be protected. The rise of the Cold War devoted unprecedented funds to the defense budget. Anti-communist propaganda created an underlying hum of paranoia. And the launch of Sputnik sent Americans scrambling to improve education—

for its white children. Early efforts to secure civil rights for black citizens, such as the 1954 U.S. Supreme Court decision to end school segregation resulted in little change in the lives of African-Americans.

But by the time John F. Kennedy began campaigning for the presidency, the country was riding high on a wave of enthusiasm about the future and hope for positive change for all Americans. Much of that hope was placed on the shoulders of young people, as the largest generation in the history of the United States was coming of age.

Alvin Eurich saw what was on the horizon. From his office at the Ford Foundation in New York City, he knew that the baby boom generation would soon lead to unprecedented numbers of college students, and new facilities would be needed to educate them. As one of Ford's grant-making staff, Eurich had suggested that the foundation board appropriate $100,000 to support efforts around the country to start new colleges. He said that the need for new colleges was also an opportunity to improve postsecondary education, arguing that, historically, "every major development in American higher education came through the establishment of new institutions, rather than through the established institutions." The board saw the need and the value and approved the use of funds to help start new, innovative colleges.[23]

When Hunter Blakely arranged a meeting with Eurich, he discovered that the Ford Foundation was intrigued by his description of a high-quality, vision-driven, liberal arts college in Florida. Eurich soon gave a $25,000 start-up grant to Florida

Presbyterian College. (Three other start-up colleges, none of which still exists today, also got $25,000 grants.) Some of the money was used to send Bill Kadel and Jack Bevan on their tour of innovative college programs throughout the country.

Kadel is quoted in a 1958 newspaper article as saying, "A God-fearing man has nothing to fear from scholarship. Man only discovers God's truths." While not an academic scholar himself and clearly hired as FPC's first president in order to represent the college to the church community, Kadel's discoveries of God's truths in his own life had led him down several unexpected paths, of which college president was just the latest.

Born in 1913 in Gettysburg, Pennsylvania, William H. Kadel was the seventh of nine children. His father, John, was a mill worker as a youngster but was able to attend school through the eighth grade and later became a postman. When he moved to Gettysburg with his large family, he opened a shop in the town square selling homemade candy, and he eventually became a Civil War battlefield guide. He also involved his children in growing gladiolas in their backyard as a cash crop. This would be the beginning of Bill's lifelong love of gardening.

Almost all the Kadel children attended Gettysburg College. The family loaned each child the tuition money, and he or she was expected to pay it back after graduation, so the funds could be used for another child's tuition. Bill, who graduated from college in 1935, also participated in the ROTC program to help with his expenses.

He decided to become a minister when he was a teenager.

While walking home from church one evening during a storm, Kadel stumbled over a bushel basket in the dark. He remembers, "I told myself then that there were a lot of people stumbling over things they couldn't see, that maybe I could help them have light. From that moment on, I began directing my life to that."[24]

After college Kadel attended Western Theological Seminary in Pittsburgh. In 1936 he married a Pennsylvania girl he had met at church camp, Katharine "Kay" Naylor. She claims he promised her he would always be a small-town preacher. God had other plans.

After completing his seminary degree in 1939 and preaching for small churches in Ohio and Pennsylvania, Kadel was drafted into the army air force in 1941 to be a chaplain for the war effort. With his ROTC background he came in as a first lieutenant and was used to train other chaplains in the routines of army life. He was soon sent to Drew Field in Tampa, Florida. Kay and their two children came with him, and a third child was born in Tampa. Although Kadel was ordered overseas five times, something always prevented his leaving at the last minute. Kay guesses it was Bill's commanding officer, who had a drinking problem, who requested Kadel stay stateside to help him.

While still in the army, Kadel became the substitute minister at Palma Ceia Presbyterian Church in Tampa. The minister's post was vacant, so the church members invited the Kadels to move into the furnished manse. When the war ended, church elders asked Kadel to become their permanent minister, but he had not yet been discharged. Kay recalls an elder saying, "We could phone Washington and get you relieved of your duty." But Kadel refused. Finally, in the fall of 1945, he was discharged, and the church called.

The Kadel family stayed on at Palma Ceia for the next eight years. During this time the church grew by over sixteen hundred members and built a new sanctuary and education building. Kadel also took a leave of absence to study for a doctor of theology degree, which he completed in 1951 at Union Seminary in Richmond. That same year Kay gave birth to their fourth and last child, Mary, who would eventually attend Florida Presbyterian College.

Bill Kadel's move from Palma Ceia Presbyterian to the First Presbyterian Church in Orlando was a kind of tug-of-war. Kadel was not sure he wanted to leave Tampa, but the Orlando church was a good career opportunity. Almost one hundred members of the Tampa church protested his leaving at a meeting of the Presbytery during which Bill's placement would be decided. In addition, a telegram asking him to remain in Tampa was signed by 464 members of his congregation. But the Presbytery approved the move, so, Kay remembers, "It was now up to Bill. . . . He came home, and he was crying. He just didn't know what to do." After a church elder impatiently pushed him to make up his mind, Bill found his resolve and announced his decision to accept the Orlando post. He was forty years old.

No doubt the growth of the Orlando church during Kadel's five-year tenure echoed the growth of Florida. But those who came once often came to stay. They not only found an "unbelievably fantastic preacher" (as Carolyn Hall said of him), but they found a minister who was approachable; even young people outside of the church came to him for advice.

"I've never seen a man who so completely practices what he preaches," said his secretary, Emma Conboy, to a news reporter. She described Kadel as "modest, with simple tastes" and "tough when that's necessary." She mentioned that her secretary's group had voted him "Boss of the Year" in 1957.

Doug Barnes, a member of the church, was quoted in the *St. Petersburg Times* when Kadel's move to FPC was announced: "There are few ministers in the world as good as this one. Before he came here, our church was just an ordinary church. Then this ball of fire came and changed all our lives, changed everything. He not only saved souls, he saved lives. This town will suffer, losing him. It isn't just a minister leaving."[25]

In his office in the Orlando church Kadel had a plaque that read: "The world has yet to see what God will do with a man fully consecrated to Him." When he was interviewed by the *St. Petersburg Times* about the new college he would be heading up, he said, "I ask people to prove their love of God by giving of their time and talent, to honor Him by giving self. That's the challenge I will present to St. Petersburg and to Florida, in constructing this college. And this is the philosophy, the spirit, we will attempt to instill in the students of Florida Presbyterian College."[26]

In the summer of 1958 Kadel left the pastor's office at the church and opened a temporary office for the college in an empty storefront in Orlando. A local bank loaned him some furniture. The board of trustees gave him twenty-five dollars as a petty cash fund.

His secretary from First Presbyterian went with him. On their first day Kadel asked, "Well, what do we need to start a college?"

Conboy said, "Paper and pencils would be a good start." So Kadel reached in his pocket and handed her some of that petty cash to buy office supplies.

While it may have been an inauspicious beginning, Kadel remembers that the change in his career quickly altered the way people treated him. "I was quite impressed with the power of the college presidency," he said later. "That change from being a pastor of a church to being a college president had tremendous implications. I went to New York and sought appointments with foundation leaders and corporate leaders and, in every case, was welcomed into their offices. These individuals showed great interest in what we were doing. It wasn't me that they were receiving into their offices, but it was a college president. This both amazed me and amused me."[27]

Although he may have been a college president for only a few weeks, Kadel quickly impressed influential men with his ideas. Kadel's early vision, as outlined for a newspaper reporter in 1958, called for "well-rounded" graduates who are "vocationally qualified and spiritually consecrated." The future college would be "sending the graduates out into society with the finest kind of academic preparation and loyalty to the highest ideals known to man, as evidenced by Christian revelation." These graduates will be "infiltrating the community life of Florida, and strengthening the state's . . . moral and spiritual fiber." Said Kadel, "We will try to give each student the basic conviction of what is right and wrong. We will try to impress on him his responsibility to these convictions, the responsibility of each individual to take a stand for right, even if he stands alone." He also emphasized freedom of choice for students in what they choose to believe as they learn: "This is the great freedom that God gave to man.

God could have made us puppets. Instead, he gave us the power to make a choice."

Kadel's plan also called for Christian faculty who envisioned their "vocation as a call from God to deal with His people." And he hoped the new campus would be planned with Florida's natural beauty in mind: "Why should a Florida student study surrounded by four walls?"[28]

For all that he was able to articulate an early vision, Kadel was talking in vague generalities. In 1958 he still had no faculty, no students, not even any other staff besides his secretary. And even if he did, he had no place to put them. Not only did Florida Presbyterian College have no campus; it did not even have a city to call home.

CHAPTER 4

Engaging the Public

Where there is no vision, the people perish.

Proverbs 29:18a King James

The Suwannee Hotel in downtown St. Petersburg had decked out its banquet hall with all the trimmings for a large and festive luncheon. But this gathering in September 1958 was not a party. In the room were more than one hundred citizens and the news media hosting the site selection committee of the board of trustees of the new Florida Presbyterian College. Important business leaders, the mayors of St. Pete and Tampa, the pastor of the First Presbyterian Church of St. Petersburg, the president of St. Petersburg Junior College, and others were there to attest to the quality of the community and its commitment to helping raise the funds the college would need to open its doors.[29]

Twenty-nine invitations to FPC had come from Florida communities that wanted the college in their cities. The site selection committee had begun its work in June and quickly narrowed the list to four possibilities: Ocala, St. Petersburg, Orlando, and Sarasota.

The St. Petersburg Committee of 100, a group of businessmen and community leaders established in 1956 to try to attract the University of South Florida to St. Pete (USF opened in Tampa in 1960), came back together to present the most compelling opportunity for Florida Presbyterian College. First, it offered the college 170 acres of land on Boca Ciega Bay in south St. Pete for the building of the new campus. This site (west of U.S. Highway 19 and bordered by Frenchman's Creek) would make FPC the first college or university in the state with a waterfront campus. St. Pete also promised that at least one hundred more acres could be pumped in from the bay to enlarge the site.

Second, St. Petersburg offered a temporary campus so classes could begin before the college was built. The city would make available, rent free, the former maritime base at Bayboro Harbor, a group of buildings near downtown St. Pete built by the U.S. government during World War II.

Third, and perhaps most important, St. Petersburg staged this stunning show of support for the college from every sector of the community. Unlike the other three cities, which hosted the site selection committee at private meals with a few local leaders, St. Petersburg used the event at the Suwannee Hotel to clinch the deal. The FPC board of trustees voted unanimously in September 1958 to build the college in St. Petersburg.

That same month Kadel and Emma Conboy moved from their store-front office in Orlando to the maritime base in St. Pete. Kadel would (perhaps unknowingly) choose the former chaplain's office for the president's office.

Within a month a Washington, DC–based group, Protestants and Other Americans United for the Separation of Church and State, called St. Pete's gift of land to a church-affiliated college unconstitutional and threatened to sue. Enter Philip Lee, the board chairman and railroad executive. Skilled at financial deals, he arranged a complicated scheme to provide the college with clear title to the land without making it a gift from the city. Part of the deal included his company giving the college some land it owned in downtown St. Petersburg that the city wanted for a parking lot at its minor league baseball field. The college deeded this site to the city and then was able to pay off a non-interest-bearing note that the college had taken to buy the campus land. Many people later wrote FPC's leaders to commend the board for not contesting the complaint and for living up to the principle of the separation of church and state.

Meanwhile, word was getting out on a national scale that something exciting was happening in higher education in Florida. Wherever Blakely traveled to education conferences, people wanted know about the new college. Newspapers all over the country wrote articles about the proposed college and its new president. Letters from interested faculty began pouring in.

Then word also got out that another Presbyterian college was simultaneously being planned for Florida, and the public became confused. The Presbyterian Church, U.S.A., which had its own national Division of Higher Education, was reading the trends in the same way as Hunter Blakely and the Presbyterian Church, U.S. As a result, they announced plans to found a Presbyterian college in Winter Haven.

The history by which it happened that two different Presbyterian groups would be proposing simultaneous new colleges in Florida is directly related to FPC's subsequent early crisis over integration. Not surprisingly, events can be traced back to the Civil War.

The Presbyterian Church in the U.S.A. (also known as the "Northern" church) was established in America around 1640. The Presbyterian Church, U.S. (also known as the "Southern" church), split from its parent group in 1861 in conjunction with the South's secession from the Union. Indeed, the Southern church was originally called the Presbyterian Church of the Confederate States of America until the war ended in 1865. At its first General Assembly in December 1861, the Southern church even entered into record a lengthy "Address to the Churches of Jesus Christ throughout the Earth" in which the church "utterly refused to make slaveholding a sin" and stated that "human rights are not a fixed, but a fluctuating quantity."[30]

Over the ensuing century the Southern church found many reasons to remain separate from the Northern church, including that the latter was committed to racial integration. But as civil rights issues heated up, membership within the Southern church began to divide along the lines of racial attitudes. While in 1950 the Southern General Assembly ratified a statement that segregation in public schools was wrong, many of its member churches opposed this action. Even as late as 1958, the year of FPC's founding, local presbyteries in the South asked the assembly to abolish its Council on Christian Relations because it opposed segregation.[31] (The Southern and Northern churches would eventually reunite in 1983 as the Presbyterian Church [U.S.A.], but not without dissent from the South's most conservative churches, many of which withdrew from the new organization.)

Throughout its existence the Southern church remained much smaller (about 830,000 members in 3,875 churches in 1958) than the Northern church (almost 3 million members in 8,362 churches in 1958). And Presbyterian congregations that aligned themselves with the Northern church existed in the southern states. But because Florida was in the South, the Northern church had many fewer members in Florida in the 1950s (about 25,000) compared to 70,000 in the Southern church. In 1958 Pinellas County, which included St. Pete, had about 2,200 members of the Northern group and about 7,250 members of the Southern group.[32]

The smaller membership, however, did not keep the Northern church in Florida from recognizing the opportunity to establish a college there. Meanwhile, the Northern and Southern churches had been urged by their leaders to seek areas of cooperation. Other Presbyterian colleges in Kentucky, Missouri, and West Virginia were being cosponsored by both churches.

So, before the FPC board of trustees was even formed, Blakely and his counterpart with the Northern church, Fay Campbell, began talking about a cooperative effort. They brought together representatives of both college planning groups for a meeting in Orlando, at which Philip Lee (of the Southern church, who would later be elected FPC's board chairman) was present. His memories of this time are instructive, if rather troubling:

> At that time the board members in the Southern church preponderantly were opposed to any union with the so-called Northern church, unless certain restrictions were met, and I might say the major one involved was that of not having the black people in our makeup of the new college. And as a matter of fact, the Southern group was determined that it was to be a segregated school. So we went to this meeting in Orlando and at the very beginning of the

51

meeting I recall that Mr. Fay Campbell made the statement he did not believe that it was possible to really and truly educate young people in any school that was not fully integrated. And after this statement the Southern group, more or less, let that be the signal that the chip had been knocked off of their shoulder. To say the least, it was not a very agreeable meeting and it accomplished, frankly, nothing other than the fact that each group understood how the other one felt on this subject.

After the FPC board was formed, Campbell requested another meeting, which the Southern group agreed to because, says Lee, "we realized the more we got into this proposition [of a new college], we needed all the help that we could get." During the meeting, which lasted past midnight and seemed like a positive step toward merging the two churches' efforts, the issue of integration never came up.

Lee walked Campbell back to his hotel that night to ask if he had changed his mind on the "Negro situation." Lee reports that Campbell stated, "Mr. Lee, I don't know what the answer is, [but] the only conclusion I have reached is that I, Fay Campbell, certainly don't have the answer and I don't propose to muddy the waters in establishing this new college by injecting this matter of which I find I am very ignorant about."[33]

The integration issue was not resolved between the two churches. It appears to have been swept under the rug in the eager rush to move ahead with a single, unified, strong proposal for a Presbyterian college in Florida.

Kadel—who had been educated in the Northern church— took a fence-sitting position on the issue early on. Anxious not to let the matter interfere with the college's development, he wanted to keep all options open to avoid alienating any side. On April 10, 1959, he told two hundred St. Pete citizens at a fund-raising campaign meeting that the issue of race "has not been faced because the general stipulations concerning enrollment have not been spelled out. The final decision rests with the board of trustees. . . . They all know the problem confronting us. They will make their decision as Floridians and Christians."[34]   Yet, according to Ashby Johnson's recollection, Kadel told the founding faculty of FPC (none of whom supported segregation) that he "would not serve as a president of a segregated institution and that the only reason there was nothing in the charter was because it was clearly presumed that it would be integrated."[35]

The officers of the boards of the two colleges met officially on September 15, 1958, with Francis Rosecrance (the consultant on the feasibility study) serving as presiding officer. The group voted in favor of a merger that would "insure the perpetual operation and control of the college by the two Presbyterian Synods of Florida." They agreed to keep Kadel as president and to make Robert M. Pratt (of the Northern church) vice president in charge of development. The board of trustees would be made up of representatives from both churches. While they would be breaking a commitment to Winter Haven, the representatives of the Northern church agreed that St. Petersburg would be an acceptable site for the college.

Kadel adjourned the meeting "with a prayer of thanksgiving to Almighty God for his presence and guidance in the deliberations of the meeting."[36]

With the church sponsorship, board membership, and location settled, Kadel and the board began the never-ending task of raising money for the college. The commitment of the citizens of St. Petersburg and Pinellas County was key to the initial fund drive. A local campaign to raise $2.5 million began in January 1959. Half of that total had been pledged by April and most of the rest by May. About 40 percent of the budget for the college in the early years would come from Pinellas County citizens and businesses. A second campaign to raise a million dollars from outside of St. Petersburg began in May 1959.

One large gift was the Florida-style mansion of Ed T. Lewis, given by his family. Located on three acres at Sixth Street and 34th Avenue South, with a small orange grove and 224 feet of waterfront, the property was worth $200,000 at the time. The house was eventually sold by the college, and the Lewis family requested that the funds from the sale be applied toward the new president's home that was to be built on the FPC campus. When the president's home was eventually completed, it was named "Lewis House" in honor of that gift.

Kadel was certainly experienced at fund-raising among church people, but he also showed skill reaching out to business leaders and community big-wigs. "He could quote the Bible at the right time with the right person," says Tom West, FPC's first director of admissions. "And he could go into a Lions group and almost win them over just because he was so humble and sincere and in no way haughty or acting as if he were better than anyone else."

Presbyterians accounted for another 40 percent of the early budget, including the direct support of the two Presbyterian Synods at around $400,000 per year. When he was not at meetings with local citizens, Kadel spent much of his time traveling to Presbyterian churches all over the state to get church members on board. Speaking in pulpits in his robes, in church basements over potluck suppers, and in church libraries to small-town elders, he talked of God's plan for this college. He described a modern campus on the water with some of the best faculty in the country teaching society's future leaders. He promised an outstanding liberal arts college where students of all faiths, or even no faith, would be challenged to discover not only a core of knowledge but also moral truths, the values for good decision making.

Kadel later recounted that the first problem with fund-raising for a brand-new college was persuading people that the founders meant business. Church members were more familiar with church colleges that started in someone's house with a dozen students. "To get people to believe us, to believe that we were serious when we said that you could begin a college and be great the day you opened, was in itself a very tough job. . . There were so many people who said we couldn't do what we were doing."[37]

But as Kadel described the character of the institution, people in and outside the church got caught up in the vision. "The base, in the beginning, was a consequence of Dr. Kadel's capacity to engage donors and the church in this exciting idea of bringing to Florida a distinguished liberal arts college," recalls Billy Wireman. "See, Florida didn't have that. Rollins [in Winter Park] was the closest thing to it at that time. But Florida was not known for a lot of great universities. . . . And to sell the people who cared about the state and who cared about the church on the idea of, in the name of the church, doing something, would be very special. And he was second to none in doing that."

Wireman continues, "He was just a man who had a vision.

One of his most famous, most frequently used quotes is, 'Where there is no vision, the people perish.' I've used it a thousand times, and he believed in it. He believed in what he was doing, he had a passion for it and had the ability to engage others in that vision."

Public relations may not have been the well-oiled profession it is today, but FPC's early leadership understood the power of it. When the editor of the *St. Petersburg Times*, Nelson Poynter, suggested the college establish a "Charter Alumni Association" by giving out honorary alumni status to individuals whose support could help the college, President Eisenhower was somehow pinpointed as the ideal first alumnus.

Perhaps it was Representative William C. Cramer, a Republican from Florida, who arranged a brief meeting in the Oval Office in April 1959. Cramer, Kadel, and Lee spent about twenty minutes with President Eisenhower. Kadel later recounted that he and the president fell into an intense discussion about the state of higher education and the important role good colleges should play in society. The two men also talked about their shared affiliation with Gettysburg (where the president had a farm). The group spent more time with the president than they had expected he could give them.

Kadel and Lee presented Eisenhower with a large scroll, embossed with FPC's new seal—a circle containing a cross inside a star accented by orbital rings—which announced his enrollment as the first charter alumnus of Florida Presbyterian College. Official photographs were snapped, and the *St. Petersburg Times* ran a story about it the next day.

Florida's governor, LeRoy Collins, became the second charter alumnus, and other honors would go to individuals who had contributed "time and talent" to the early campaign, including anyone who gave at least $1,250. The argument for charter alumni was that established colleges have a base of alumni to count on for support, but FPC would not have that for quite a while.

At the same time, the college was advertising its founding and search for students and faculty in such publications as *Time*, *All-Florida Magazine*, *Presbyterian Life*, and *Presbyterian Journal*. Radio and television news spots as well as newspaper articles covered the unfolding details about the new college. With each passing month board members and staff made public appearances and spoke about FPC to countless groups. In just the month of April 1960, FPC representatives gave forty-one talks about the college.

Meanwhile, John Satterfield began planning an Artist-Lecturer Series for students and the public to be held at Pasadena Community Church during the college's first year. He remembers telling Bevan, "We've got a town full of retirees here. These people are just sitting around with nothing to do. They want to be entertained when they can. Many of them are Yankees and pretentious as they can be about what's cultural and what isn't. Let's get some real culture down here, and let them pay for the tickets, and we can give the art to our students and it doesn't cost us a thing." Opera singers Roberta Peters and William Warfield, actor Basil Rathbone, guitarist Andrés Segovia, and rocket scientist Wernher von Braun were among those who accepted Satterfield's invitation.

Fund-raising and promotion of the new institution focused not only on the educational vision and impact of FPC but also on the needs of a campus yet to be built. Kadel knew all about finding money to build buildings, and he gave particular emphasis to conjuring in the minds of potential donors concrete images of classrooms and science labs, offices and auditoriums, dormitories and dining halls, library and chapel.

The land itself—the acres of undeveloped shoreline on Boca Ciega Bay—made the vision easier to sell. In today's Florida, where almost all waterfront property is developed at exorbitant prices, it is staggering to realize that as recently as 1940 no one stepped up to buy this land for just the taxes owed. The delinquent taxpayer, Roy S. Hanna, had bought the property in 1903. While he was one of St. Petersburg's important early citizens and eventually postmaster under President Hoover, he owned more land than he could afford as taxes rose. In 1940 the city took control of the property, which had never been developed beyond modest shacks, a small fishing business, and short-lived farming.

The land consisted mostly of native scrub, saw grass and sandspurs, tall pines and stately live oaks, and sandy beaches on the bay. Mangroves growing over the inland water sheltered wading egrets and herons. A single squatter was living on the land when the college took it over. Ashby Johnson recalls that, while the man had no legal rights to it, the college gave him money and helped him relocate.

To those with more interest in Florida's future growth than in Florida's natural resources, the site was ripe for clusters of buildings designed around an academic enterprise. It could also be nearly doubled in size by dredging sand from the bottom of the bay and piling it up behind sturdy seawalls.

Few gave thought at that time to the preservation of the coastal ecosystem. Although one founding faculty member, George Reid, FPC's first professor of biology, raised objections to the landfill based on the negative environmental impact, everyone else was focused on the advantages of the additional land. Satterfield remembers this controversy as one of the first conflicts between faculty and the board. Apparently, Reid wrote an article for the *St. Petersburg Times* about how coastal developments throughout Florida were ruining marine life by damaging the mangrove swamps and other habitats.

"Oh, the board of trustees hit the ceiling," Satterfield recalls. "Some of them were developers. They wanted Reid fired. So I guess Bill Kadel ran into his first academic freedom thing, and, for him, with his background, that was just an absurd confrontation. How did this ever happen? But, boy, he stuck to his guns. He said, 'My understanding of academic freedom has grown a great deal since I have come to be associated with these people that I'm working with here, and I'll tell you right now that there's nothing in the world that can limit what one of our biologists has to say about the marine life on the coast, and you're going to have to live with that because that's his right.'"

Despite Reid's objections, the area around the campus was filled in to create more acreage. The job was done as a donation from a local contractor.

By the fall of 1959 the FPC president and board had architectural drawings to show off to potential donors. Although much of their original plans were not implemented as first designed, key elements of these drawings are evident in the college campus to this day: the first library at the top of a U-shaped road, the chapel on a bridge between two ponds, a quadrangle of academic buildings, dorms in clusters near the water, boat slips on Frenchman's Creek.

The college also now had policies for staff salaries, holidays and vacations, health insurance, retirement plans, student scholarships, and sabbatical leave for faculty. And FPC had the beginning of a faculty, as Bevan's recruits came to the maritime base in December 1959 to begin planning the curriculum. What the college did not have was students.

CHAPTER 5

We Need Students

We probably won't be able to say exactly what took place with
the formation and development of this college. Miracles which
include supernatural forces seem strained, unnecessary, and finally
questionable to me. But what about surpassingly remarkable
outcomes for attempts to create within nature?

John Satterfield

When the phone rang in Tom West's home in Nashville, he
was not thinking of the letter he had written only a few days ago,
just on the spur of the moment, to the founders of a new college
in Florida. But he had hardly said hello before Jack Bevan's
urgent enthusiasm was rushing out of the receiver. "We need
students," he told West. "We've been busy finding the faculty,
raising money, planning the curriculum. But we don't have a
director of admissions yet. Why don't you come down here and
talk with us?"

It was the summer of 1959. That May FPC's board had set
September 1960 as the date to open the college—on the
temporary maritime base campus—and begin classes. Only a
freshman class would be accepted for the first year, and an
additional class would be added in the three subsequent years.

While letters were pouring in from potential faculty, nobody was actively recruiting students to apply.

Bevan considered it "one of the luckiest days when I found Tom West, or when he found me." West was working for the state of Tennessee at the time. He had never worked in college admissions. But he had a doctorate in psychology and experience in starting new programs. Something about his letter had captured Bevan's attention, and FPC was about to capture Tom.

"They flew me down," West remembers, "and they hired me that day. They didn't even do a search. They just hired me. I was a Presbyterian, I knew Florida, I had the doctorate degree, I was involved in teaching, and I was a pretty decent fellow. So they took a chance, just like I guess everyone else was taking a chance with them." In addition to finding the first students for FPC, West would be a professor of psychology and the first dean of men.

Thomas J. West was thirty-five when the college opened and the only Florida native on the faculty. Born in Winter Haven during a hurricane ("I came with a lot of hot air," Tom says), he was the son of an M.D. from Johns Hopkins Medical School who had come to Florida with his wife and two teenage daughters to retire on a small orange grove. Tom's father was a Quaker and a stiff, orderly man. A new baby boy was not exactly in his plans. Nor was his long, painful death from colon cancer when Tom was still a preschooler.

Tom's mother, who was in her mid-forties when Tom was born, tried to run the grove by herself, took in borders, and did her best to raise her three children as solid Christians. She was a pillar of the First Presbyterian Church in Winter Haven. Tom says he always felt he had three mothers, given the way his two older sisters helped to care for him.

He joined the army air corps right out of high school, but the war was coming to an end, so he was discharged "at the convenience of the government" and went to Davidson College on the GI Bill. He thought about becoming a doctor, like his father, but when he took his first psychology course, he knew he had found his calling. He earned a master's degree in psychology at the University of North Carolina and then helped start a new public high school in Charlotte, where he was the director of counseling. "I liked beginning things," says West. After two years there he began working on his doctorate at Vanderbilt University in Nashville.

During this time his two sisters died of cancer, and his mother was killed in a car accident. So, by the age of thirty, West was alone in the world. "There are tender-minded and tough-minded people, according to William James," he says, "and I became a tender-minded person, which means that I was never going to be a tough, macho man, but I would be a man who could work with compassion and empathy, so it was perfect for going into counseling." West began teaching psychology at Vanderbilt and the University of Tennessee and then was hired to start a new program in mental health education for the state of Tennessee.

"But I was a Florida Cracker, and I kept hearing there were things going on down in Florida dealing with a brand-new Presbyterian college. And I was a very strong Presbyterian." By October 1959 West and his pregnant wife had moved to St. Petersburg. Later that fall their son, Jim, was baptized by Bill Kadel in the first religious ceremony on the interim campus.

When his faculty colleagues met him later, they were not surprised that this young, personable man—with his warm eyes, soft-spoken gentleness, and intense way of listening to others—would have been able to convince high school seniors to come to an unaccredited, barely formed, not yet built institution. West was known to be upbeat, optimistic, and passionate about the college's future. But the effort that resulted in FPC's first freshman class of more than 150 students was hardly a breeze for West.

When he first arrived to begin his duties in October 1959, he was given a pile of "IBM cards" by the director of development, Robert Pratt (who had been selected for that position when the two churches merged their efforts; he would not last long at FPC). West remembers Pratt claimed, "Oh, we'll have no trouble getting students. I have nine hundred cards with the names of people who are interested in being students here." Most of the cards had come from the Presbyterian churches in Florida.

"Well, I looked at the cards," West remembers, "and all they said was, 'Would you be interested in knowing about Florida Presbyterian College, a new Presbyterian college that is going to be developed in Florida? Check yes or no and then sign your name and indicate what year you are in high school.' Most of them were ninth- and tenth-graders, very few seniors. I looked at them, and I just turned white, because I knew then that we had a job to do."

The college asked prominent Presbyterian and citrus grower, Ben Hill Griffin (whose name would later grace the new campus chapel), to donate a used Ford automobile for West to take on his recruiting trips. "I got in that Ford and with just pictures of what the campus looked like, a little bit from Jack Bevan on what the curriculum would be, and a few ideas about what kind of faculty, I headed out and started going to every high school in the state."

West recruited seven days a week from then until April 1960 and logged about thirty thousand miles on that Ford. Almost every evening he would call Jack Bevan and ask, "What have you done now?" He needed regular updates on decisions about the curriculum, faculty, application requirements, scholarship funds, and so on. "It was evolving the whole time."

West would also check in with his new secretary, Eleanor Pugh, a short, no-nonsense Canadian who had just started working at FPC—one of the very few early staff members. Pugh would work with West at the college for the rest of her career. Describing her big heart, ability to keep things organized, and intuition about students' needs, West says today, "Eleanor Pugh was very, very important in my life."

When West talked with high school students, he shared with them the vision for FPC that he had heard from Bevan and Kadel. He also had a set of artist's renderings of the new campus that highlighted the waterfront, modern buildings, and small, community-oriented dormitories. "And I kept saying, 'If you'd really like to get in on something that's just beginning and feel like you're doing something truly important and, at the same time, get one of the most unique, edge-of-the-forest kinds of an education, then you might want to come to Florida Presbyterian College.' And I would get students all excited at college nights and everything, and then they would go home and tell their parents, 'I want to go to Florida Presbyterian College.' And their parents would say, 'What? It's not there yet? It's not accredited? You want to go there when we can get you into Stetson or Florida Southern or a state university?' And then I would get shot down. I'd never hear from them again."

For a while more applications were coming in from potential faculty members than from potential students. By May 1960, 260 students had applied, and 110 had so far been accepted (slightly more girls than boys).[38] "Somehow or other, we got 155 students to start," says West.

The original plan had been for four hundred freshmen, but when the administration realized how little time they had, how few real leads, and how few qualified seniors were still deciding where to go to college, they were thrilled to get as many as they did. The student-faculty ratio for the first year was a luxurious six to one.

While forty-three students in that first class came from nineteen different states and one from Japan, most were from Florida, including thirty-four from St. Petersburg. Of the total student body 73 percent were Presbyterians. Eighty-two percent of those who were accepted decided to enroll.

One of those Florida students was Carolyn Hall (now Horton), from Orlando. She knew about FPC because her family went to the First Presbyterian Church where Bill Kadel had been the minister. In fact, her mother was employed as a secretary at the church, after Carolyn's father had walked out on the family. "My mother had never finished college," says Hall. "But she expected that I would go and said I better make good grades to get a scholarship. One motivation for me to graduate from college was so I never had to work like my mother did for the pennies she got."

Carolyn, a petite blonde with a sweet, round face, was a self-defined "good girl." The oldest of four children, she helped take care of her siblings after school while her mother was at work. She felt like a "misfit" in high school, even though she was the president of the Honor Society and manager of the swim team, so church became the center of her social life. She was a member of the church choir and a leader in the church youth group. When she took French in high school, she decided then and there to become a foreign language teacher. "I had an awful French teacher, and I thought, 'The kids of the world deserve better than this.'" She also became president of Future Teachers of America.

Hall began hearing about FPC early in its development. "It was very exciting," she remembers. "It was a pioneering Christian thing." Hall saw the opportunity to attend FPC as a "chance to dovetail a spiritual life with an academic one." She was enticed by the idea of being one of the first students and saw it as a chance to start something that was going to be excellent. "I looked at other colleges, but my memory is that I didn't apply anywhere else."

Beginning with a letter from Tom West in October 1959, Hall received eighteen letters from the college over the next eight months. She was encouraged to "drop by the Admissions Office" in St. Pete, she was invited to apply for a scholarship, and Kadel even wrote her in January 1960 to say he was glad to hear she had applied. The personal attention meant a lot to Hall. She has saved these letters to this day.

Hall visited the interim campus. After landlocked Orlando with its orange groves and sandspurs, Carolyn was taken with the waterfront setting. She also remembers meeting Tom West (whom she calls "J. Tommy") and thinking he was "almost too nice—you wondered whether he was real." She was pleased to learn of plans for good foreign language professors, and she was even more pleased to receive scholarships from the college (and help from people at her church) to afford the tuition and fees, which totaled fifteen hundred dollars.

"I was enthralled," says Hall, "really caught up in the whole idea." She could hardly wait until September.

One of the few students who came from out of state was Grover Wrenn, of the small town of Siler City, North Carolina. A skinny guy with a pronounced southern drawl, he was the oldest of three sons of a physician father (who was also the town mayor) and a nurse mother who quit work to raise the boys. They were charter members of the only Presbyterian church in town. Grover became a youth leader with the Presbyterians at the state level.

He attended a small high school with limited resources, and he didn't have to study hard to do well. For an added challenge he spent six weeks in the summer after his junior year taking a college chemistry course at Western Carolina College in Cullowhee. "This course exposed me to far and away the best teaching I had ever experienced," Wrenn remembers. The professor was Dexter Squibb.

"He lived to teach chemistry," says Wrenn. "He rewrote his class notes three times a year, always striving to improve ways to create that spark of understanding in your eye as he taught you.

The high school science I had taken was merely descriptive. This course gave me insights into understanding the foundations of the world of chemistry, and it was a thrilling intellectual experience." While Wrenn was in that class, Squibb was talking with Bevan about becoming the first chemistry professor at Florida Presbyterian College. "He shared that with some of us in his class," says Wrenn, "and talked about the idea of the school."

While going to a church-related or Presbyterian college was not a requirement to Wrenn, he saw that as an "additional attraction to FPC."

In his senior year Grover convinced his mother to drive down to St. Petersburg with him and visit the school during a "scholarship weekend." Before he left the interim campus, he had been offered an honor scholarship, and he knew he was going to accept.

"The people I met just created a sense of excitement and desire to be part of this new venture. . . . It was a compellingly appealing story. I mean, the commitment, the enthusiasm. People have asked me at times, 'Didn't you worry about going to a school that wasn't accredited yet?' It never crossed my mind. . . . What I heard was the story of the new beginning."

The college's almost desperate bid to secure a founding freshman class created an interesting mix of students. While the vision for the school was for "outstanding" students—the cream of the crop who really wanted to be challenged by a rigorous curriculum and new ideas—many of the best high school seniors had already decided to attend established, prestigious colleges and universities.

"Towards the end, they opened up the scholarships," West remembers. "They said, 'We'll find the money. Just go find the students.' So I could go and almost buy some students away from some other places."

West also looked for high-ability, low-achieving students who were not getting accepted elsewhere but whose test scores and teacher recommendations suggested they had a lot of potential. West remembers teachers would say, "I sure wish this student would catch fire, because he or she could do so well." Tom believed FPC was going to be the kind of place to ignite students' learning.

"We ended up with students who were either brilliant and came with all kinds of scholarship money and were excited about this being a real vision for them, or they were high potential, low achievers," says West. He began a summertime "Low Achievers Program" that taught such students how to study and how to read and write better. "We did well with those," he says. "In fact, we'd bring some of these risky students in, and their graduation rate was as high as some of the students who were just high achievers in every respect."

FPC's faculty was not always understanding of the decision to allow less-than-stellar students into the demanding learning community they were envisioning. West remembers, "Some of the faculty would say, 'You mean to say that this student only has a C average in high school?' . . . Some of the faculty had to be educated about the fact that we needed this college to get going, and so we took some risks."

Bevan remembers reporting the characteristics of the first freshman class to the newly gathered faculty. "I remember putting on the board the distribution of SAT [Scholastic Aptitude Test] scores of the freshman class. We had a bimodal distribution. If you hit them in the middle, you would hit nothing. And my question was, 'Where do we hit? Do we hit in the middle at the higher end, or the middle of the lower end? There's no point in hitting the middle in the middle, because there's nobody there!' And they said, 'The higher end.' Well, we knew that hitting at the higher end meant that it was going to be very difficult for those at the lower end. . . . And some of those students had a really rough go at it the first year."[39]

Ashby Johnson later reflected, "A simple way of putting it would be to say that, of the [first] students, about half of them certainly were qualified to be there because they ranked in the 98.6% of the nation in SAT scores, and the other half were qualified because they had body temperatures of about 98.6."[40]

John Satterfield's memory of that first class was that the college had "an uncommon number of students with problems that I suppose a psychologist would call 'mild to relatively heavy neurosis'—adjustment problems—and we probably attracted people like that because they were pretty much bored with convention and wanted an opportunity to try something different: 'Well, I have been somewhat dysfunctional, somewhat dissatisfied through high school and other places. Maybe at this place I can be myself.'"[41]

Little did the first students know what the faculty had in mind for them.

CHAPTER 6

A New Adventure in Education

My Lord—we were going to revamp American higher education!
If that sounds like bitterness, it's wrong—it's not bitter. I still think
it was pretty damn sound.

Ashby Johnson

More than a decade after Florida Presbyterian College had opened its doors to students and faculty, students were given permission to plan their own May Commencement. They moved the ceremony from its traditional location at Pasadena Community Church to the grass-and-sand academic quadrangle on campus. They decided to wear different colored robes for the different departmental divisions (known by then as "collegia") and declared that they would not wear mortar boards.

Students told the faculty that they could still wear their black gowns, but they invited faculty to consider whether they would also like to dispense with the mortar boards. Bill McKee, who came to FPC in 1967 as a professor of history, remembers, "We argued this in terms of educational philosophy."

According to McKee, the more conservative faculty (largely in natural sciences and foreign languages) argued that the purpose of higher education was to train students in the traditional disciplines of the liberal arts and sciences. Therefore, everyone should wear the traditional garb.

The radicals (largely in creative arts) argued that the purpose of education was to enable students to experiment in alternative lifestyles. Therefore, the faculty should wear creative hats.

In the middle were the liberals (largely in social sciences), who argued that the purpose of higher education is to enable students to make informed and meaningful value judgments. Therefore, each professor ought to make up his or her own mind.

The middle of the road was the majority, so each faculty member was allowed to wear whatever he or she wanted. Straw hats with wide brims to protect from the Florida sun became a favorite.

McKee's story is indicative of faculty negotiations since the earliest days of the college.

On a steamy summer day in 1959 some of the first faculty of Florida Presbyterian College arrived at the maritime base on Bayboro Harbor for an intensive retreat to plan the curriculum. They would all go back to their other jobs for the next academic year, returning to St. Petersburg in December for a second planning session, and many would come back the following summer for good, to begin new positions as FPC professors.

On their way to the planning meeting they walked along a concrete seawall next to the calm green waters of Tampa Bay. They might have stopped to watch dolphins swimming by or a pelican dive for fish—things they had certainly never seen in their homes farther north. Perhaps they watched sailboats in the bay and vowed that if they got a job at FPC they would take up boating or waterskiing. Many of them eventually did.

They might have walked from one of St. Pete's old downtown hotels to the temporary campus. To some St. Pete seemed a bit dreary, uncultured, behind the times. A haven for retirees in the winter, it probably looked fairly deserted in summer. But downtown was still the center of the community's activities at that time, with huge, well-attended churches, fancy hotels, multi-floor department stores, the country's oldest open-air post office, and a baseball field that hosted major league teams during spring training.

German professor Ken Keeton remembers flying down to St. Pete from Kentucky, at Bevan's invitation. "I thought it must be the end of the earth, because I saw all these old people walking around. I stayed in a hotel where everybody was old. It was right downtown. And I thought, 'What in God's name have I gotten into?'"

If he had gone out to the sandy beaches of Indian Rocks, Treasure Island, and St. Pete Beach, he might have felt differently. At that time the beaches were rather isolated from the activity of city life. Sterling Watson (an early FPC student and later faculty member) lived in a seven-bedroom beach house with his parents and siblings for one hundred dollars a month. He remembers, "You could get up in the morning and go for a walk and never see another person."

Architecture of the city tended toward Mediterranean Revival, with stucco walls, light-pink plaster, tropical courtyards, and wrought-iron fencing. The streets were laid out in an orderly grid with Central Avenue running through the heart of downtown, dividing numbered avenues to the north and south, and crisscrossed by numbered streets beginning at 1st Street on the east (along Tampa Bay) and working up to over 75th in the west (on Boca Ciega Bay). The city was racially segregated such that residents could identify the "black part of town"—which was also the most impoverished—by the streets and avenues that bounded it.

Little development at all existed near the site of the new FPC campus on the south side of town at 34th Street and 54th Avenue South. Even by the mid-1960s the closest restaurant for students was a greasy spoon named Henry's Diner, located around 16th Avenue South. Students called it "Chez Henri."

FPC's interim campus, used until the fall of 1963, was a World War II–era naval base located near 1st Street and 5th Avenue South. A series of low-slung, gray concrete buildings, sitting on a finger of land jutting into Tampa Bay, the marina was still used by naval ships and submarines. The air was noisy with seaplanes from a nearby Coast Guard station and prop planes from the municipal airport across the street. It was not the most inspiring location to design a "new adventure in education."[42] But by the time the faculty first saw the interim campus, the buildings were being remodeled into offices, classrooms, dorm rooms, library, and cafeteria, all with a waterfront view. There were also tennis courts and a swimming pool.

And one spacious room, cooled by a new air conditioning system and filled with comfortable armchairs in a circle, awaited the new faculty who had come to decide what, and how, the college should teach.

It is 1959. FPC's founding faculty are all over thirty but under fifty. All white, and all men, they are clean-shaven with either crew cuts or slicked-back receding hairlines. Some wear black-rimmed glasses in the style of the time. They carry notebooks and pens but little else, since most of the paperwork of the college has yet to be amassed. They all swig coffee, many are smoking, and the room is buzzing with conversation. Hands gesture wildly; heads nod in emphatic agreement. Bevan shouts above the din, "Let's get started." It seems they already have.

While the work they have come to do is focused on the college's structure, requirements, and curriculum, Bevan is also getting a sense of how these men fit together as a faculty. In this and subsequent sessions they will reveal their philosophies of education, their perspectives on their disciplines, their ideas about students. And they will begin to develop alliances and friendships with one another, forging deep relationships that will grow along with the college and last for decades.

The faculty have already heard about Bevan's emphasis on interdisciplinary learning, on breaking down the divisions between departments that are typical of other colleges. FPC will have only three divisions: Humanities, History and Social Sciences, and Math and Natural Sciences.

He explains that the curriculum calls for a four-year interdisciplinary program required of all students, something Bevan does not believe is done at any other college in the country, save St. John's (whose program, based on reading the classics, he sees as quite different).[43] In the first two years all students will take "Western Civilization and Its Christian Heritage," to pursue a "critical understanding of the major attempts of man to interpret his purpose and to organize his experience through the analytic and historical study of works and institutions."[44] The third year is originally planned to study world literature but will instead become a survey course on Asia.

In the senior year all students will study "The Christian Faith and Great Issues." Says Bevan, "This course will not be designed to indoctrinate but to challenge students to think through some major social, economic, and political issues in the light of their own personal value systems—their own basic beliefs whatever they may be."[45]

Bevan tells the faculty that "the greatest unused resource in this country is the minds of young people." His objective is to stretch students, to make them reach farther than they thought they could. ("We always asked more of the students than we or they thought they could accomplish," sociologist Clark Bouwman remembers, "and, lo and behold, they did accomplish a lot of it.")

Bevan declares that FPC will have no middle-sized classes, just large lectures and small, intimate discussion groups. "Your first job as a faculty member is to teach," he reminds them. "We'd love for you to do research, we'd love for you to publish, but you're here, first of all, to teach."

Kadel is also present at the beginning of the meeting to welcome these future professors and to remind them of the tenets on which FPC is based:

In this new endeavor, we have asked, 'Can the community of faith (which is a propositional community) and the community of learning (which is an open community) really co-exist without doing violence to either one, without either one violating the integrity of the other, and each contributing something to the lifestyle of the other community as they interact and interface in the college?' With that in mind, our sense of what it means to be a church college takes on some very different meanings.

For one thing, we believe that the data that belong historically to the Christian faith are important data and cannot be left out of the curriculum. But we believe that data should be addressed with the same kind of academic integrity as any other data that constitutes any part of the curriculum. So the Core program should be designed to give a centrality to the thinking within the educational community of the meaning of Judeo-Christian faith on the whole educational and learning process.

Another is that we believe that, according to the witness of Scripture, individuals are very important people, are not to be manipulated, are to be free, and that therefore the student as person needs to be free in the community, and that means free from not only the indoctrination of religious leaders, but free from the indoctrination of educational leaders.[46]

Everyone has already agreed that FPC will not require attendance at chapel services or teach "Bible classes" as other church-related colleges often do. The Christian faith and a "lively encounter with Christianity" will be woven into the curriculum and intentions of the college throughout a student's education.

One of the primary tasks of these early faculty meetings is the design of FPC's central curricular component, "Western Civilization and Its Christian Heritage." This class, which will be required of all freshmen and sophomores, will include two to three whole-group lectures a week, plus smaller discussion seminars. Almost all the faculty, no matter what their disciplines, will help teach it. Its prominence as the core component of the curriculum earns it the moniker "Core," as in, "I've got to do my readings for Core" and "Who is lecturing in Core this week?"

The first issue the faculty discusses is what readings the course will cover. John Satterfield, the music professor and jazz musician, leans over to his Davidson colleague, Spanish professor Pedro Trakas, and whispers, "There's a tendency on the part of some of us to go to known patterns in designing this course. There's a tendency on the part of others to avoid all known patterns to the extent we can. The acceptors of hand-me-down opinion are confronted by some people who don't want to accept hand-me-down opinion. I want students to make their own opinions. But, of course, we are put in a position that we have to hand it down, because we have to select the material."

Satterfield then speaks to the group. "I earned four degrees from the University of North Carolina. And not once in all those years was I asked to read the Bible. I didn't read Freud or Marx either. I never had contact with the founding minds of Western society. At FPC, we won't have the students reading some second-rate textbook by some unknown who presumes to tell them what is important."[47]

Agreement is strong on the value of reading primary texts. But which texts and in what order?

"We're forgetting about the historical context," says history professor Bill Wilbur. "We need to bring in more of the historical context—when these books were written, what preceded them, what was going on in the world at the same time." Others argue strongly for starting with the Greeks or Hebrews and working forward through time.

Art historian John Dixon points out, "We are setting out consciously to construct a curriculum for a Christian college. It is important that this course reflect this concern both in its content and in its organization. Intellectually speaking, one of the most important characteristics of Christianity is its locus in history. God acts in history and the student ought to end up with a profound sense of history in his bones."

"Chronology is not the cementum that holds everything together," says humanities professor Howard Carter.

"It is ridiculous to say that you can't read *Hamlet* without having first read *Oedipus*," says Satterfield. "How many people have and have survived?"

Dixon and others suggest starting the course with more modern writers, like Kerouac and T. S. Eliot, and then stepping farther back in time. "Students are bored and don't learn much because we make our material boring and irrelevant," says Dixon. "And while my impression is that Jack is getting together some people who have managed to keep some of their students interested some of the time, my general observation is that the weight of American education is against it. I would like us to do better."

"I do not think," Wilbur chimes in, "that the historical or chronological organization of material in itself must cause students to fail to see any relevance or to lose interest."

Carter recommends ordering the readings from simplest to most complex and not thinking about teaching epochs. "As an artist and an existentialist I don't want to study, let alone teach, epochs; I want to teach works of art. Secondly, I want to interest students in problems and in problem solving." He suggests they just come to agreement about the list of works and let the themes of the course develop "as we discover them in the students."

Satterfield agrees. "I read Lord Tennyson in college because the course, which was to be a survey of English literature, had to have an English writer representative of each period in English literature. That is the wrong question. You start out by asking the question, 'Is the guy worth reading?'"

Ashby Johnson asks whether they should be trying to be experimental, questioning the root assumptions of what it means to provide a liberal arts education. Someone else responds that what they really need to do is get a plan down on paper, and quickly. (Ken Keeton would come to characterize the founding faculty as 90 percent flaming liberals, 5 percent conservative, and 5 percent ultra-conservative.)

"We might well sit around and talk about this until next June," Carter warns. "Whatever we decide, we and the students should all be working like hell to get as much read, listened to, seen, learned, as possible. Possible comparative scale: one year at FPC is worth four at Princeton."

Dixon adds, "And part of the purpose should be to shock students into intellectual self-consciousness. They should see that the world they live in is not a great cow to be milked for their private sustenance but a place of action and decision. If they must be prepared to see their world critically and constructively then it must be alive in their consciousness from the time they enter the school."

When the Western Civ class is finalized, the general trend is toward a chronological presentation of great works in literature, religion, the arts, history, political science, psychology, and more. But the faculty also agree that they cannot take freshmen at an untried school and start them off with the ancients. "It would have been like throwing them to the sharks," says Satterfield. "The way to grab their attention is to start with something current that they will judge as important for themselves right now."

So the first semester, organized around the theme of "tradition and dissent," requires students to read *Cry, the Beloved Country* as well as Genesis 1–11 and the Gospel according to Mark before they even arrive on campus. The fall syllabus also includes *The Catcher in the Rye*, writings by Kafka, Tennessee Williams, Dostoevsky, Joyce, and Niebuhr as well as works by Stravinsky, Brahms, Goya, and Van Gogh. Recognizing that the course should represent all disciplines, the faculty also assigned excerpts on biology, evolution, astronomy, energy, economics, mathematics, and physics. (Satterfield says he was always sorry the list of more recent works never included *To Kill a Mockingbird*. "I don't know how we missed it. It's just loaded with themes that we were emphasizing: grace, sovereignism, feminism, justice, all those.")

The second semester will begin with *The Iliad*, then *Prometheus* and *Oedipus*, move on to Plato and Aristotle, and then the Old and New Testaments. The second year of Western Civ will continue on chronologically from there.

Forty-five years later, Satterfield recalled those early planning meetings: "It took some time for us to learn that we could tease one another and greatly break the tension. That tension was heavy and omnipresent, but the debate became full of wisecracks, irony, satire, sometimes unforgivable puns as repartee."[48] (When art professor James Crane first had to give a lecture [in 1963], he was assigned to speak immediately after a lecture by Bevan. "After he was through," says Crane, "I was just absolutely blown away, and I said, 'Jack, you're a hard guy to follow.' And he said, 'I thought I was perfectly clear.'")[49]

When Johnson looked back on the planning for Western Civ, he perceived that "though we were quite innovative and experimental in the methods that we wanted to employ in teaching, our goals so far as liberal arts education was concerned were highly conventional."[50]

Bill Wilbur agrees. "I think most of the people came to feel that we were an *innovative* college, that we were not as *experimental* as some colleges that were, for example, letting students design the curriculum. But we were, I think, on the cutting edge in 1960."

Clark Bouwman remembers the curriculum for Core as "just phenomenal." He says, "Although I had just completed my Ph.D. the year before, at Illinois Wesleyan, I really was aware as I got into this course, 'Now, I'm really getting educated for the first time.' I felt I was getting my education filled in and polished off, because it wasn't specialization. I was learning all kinds of things that it seemed to me any knowledgeable person ought to have had, and that was one of the most exciting things—the self-fulfillment that took place as I got involved in that Western Heritage course."

Back in the planning meetings, Bevan is reminding the faculty that independent study will be another important part of the curriculum. He tells them about efforts to develop the library, generously sponsored by the William Luther Cobb family, which by the college's opening will already have almost 15,000 books and 175 periodical subscriptions. Bevan plans that no penalty will be charged for books returned after the due date. "I'm also very much in favor of letting students get off campus and be on their own and study on their own."

The January term (also known as interim term, winter term, and the midwinter semester) is intended to strengthen students' skills in independent study. They will be able to design their own projects, to pursue them on or off campus, or join with other students in a shared project, always with the guidance of a single professor. Bevan expects it to be "a wonderful opportunity for students starting in the freshman year to begin to learn how to do something on their own."

But independent study will not be limited only to January. Students will be encouraged to work on their own during the regular semesters and over the summer. "Proficiency rather than fulfillment of course requirements is the measure of accomplishment and admission to advanced studies," says the college handbook Bevan has developed.[51] With this in mind the college will not require students to attend classes. "The evaluation of academic progress . . . rests on a student's response to educational opportunity. . . . Our rewards and awards are for outstanding and creative work."

Grades are, therefore, going to be used "only for advisory purposes." Students will receive only H (honors), S (satisfactory), and U (unsatisfactory). (S+ and S- would be added not long after, essentially mimicking the A–F grading system.)

Bevan also tells them that he wants to avoid "point credit and cut systems that tend to give education its terminal attitude and status and make unavailable to the student many exciting learning experiences."[52] Graduation will be based on the completion of thirty-nine courses (no "credit hours" are defined), demonstrated proficiency in a foreign language, and satisfactory results on a comprehensive exam in a major field of study.

The discussion turns to teaching methods in the classroom. "I want this to be one of the most unusual educational institutions you will ever find," says psychologist Tom West. "I want a sense of shared learning. I want the students to realize that they are definitely not going to be spoon fed, that they have a big to-do in how courses form and how courses are delivered and how the academic program unfolds for them. I want them to become truly aware of where they are, what is going on in the country, how they need to be able to continue to think and learn long after they leave college. The process should definitely be on how to learn."

Satterfield adds, "Teaching is about asking the students to talk to me about what they read. It's always fascinating to hear from the students. I'm not going to just tell them what I read. In my music history course, if I stand up there and just recite to you names and dates and what they wrote and so on, that is somewhat ridiculous to me. That's all in a textbook that we can all read. I think you ought to read the history books and you ought to know what the trends are, but I think it's much more important for you to analyze a piece of music that's representative of a time, a period, a composer, and try to tell me what's going on in it. And I'll point out to you when I have more experience. If I have more experience, I'll tell you something that you should know."

Billy Wireman, the athletic director (and future college president), agrees. "That's what liberal arts education ought to be about: independent study, cohesiveness, coherence, capacity to participate, to question, defend your position, challenge others.

You can't get that from a lecture where you just take notes and play it back."

West points out, "Of course, some of them are used to being spoon fed in high school and just being told exactly what to learn and how to learn it, and this is going to be difficult for them, a lot of them. But the faculty will be constantly saying, 'Look, we're learning, too, and what do you have to say? What's your input in this, from your vantage point, from your age range?'"

"I've always taught on the discursive basis," says Bouwman. "Give and take and students expressing themselves, formulating their ideas. I've never felt the need to say, 'This is what is the truth.' I want to relate to students and learn from them."

"We want the students to learn their values," says West, "and not just have them passed down, but to struggle with them and come up with them."

Keeton emphasizes the need to support and encourage students. "It's like seeing God as beneficent and tolerant of all things. Students tend to be that way, you know, they want to be loved and not to have a lot of criticism. Faculty should be more than just teachers; they should be friends and role models for students."

"The strongest role at the college should always be the faculty-student relationships and interplay," says Bouwman. "We will prepare people for graduate school with that kind of an undergraduate emphasis, and our students will not suffer from not having a professionalized orientation, in terms of scientific research and publication."

Wilbur, who had been a Danforth Fellow previously in his career, remembers the emphasis the Danforth Foundation placed on faculty-student relations. "They encouraged faculty to entertain the students in their homes and even gave you a small stipend to pay for the expense of having meals and buying some books and so on. I always enjoyed that personally."

"I also invited students to my home at Wake Forest," says Keeton. "Fortunately, I became personal friends with a lot of students. And I've had to fail students who were very good friends. Oh, that breaks your heart."

"I've never failed anyone," says math professor Bob Meacham. "Students fail themselves if they don't try. I will be extremely generous with my time. My office door is always open. Any student who wants help can come."

The faculty meeting then turns to another familiar topic: what courses will be required. Keeton has been promised a three-year language requirement, which he will get in the early years and lament the loss of in later years. As a result of this requirement, students would often come to say, "Hey, if I've got to take three years, I might as well major." FPC would end up with a lot of language majors in its first few graduating classes.

The math professors are insistent that everyone take at least two years of mathematics or logic. The social scientists want two years of required classes from an array of choices in their field.

Of course, these possible requirements are on top of the required Core courses which take up time in every student's schedule every semester. The science faculty raise familiar objections: If we have all these liberal arts requirements for everybody, how are we going to get science majors through all the courses and lab work needed to prepare them for graduate school?

Tom West says, "I'm more on the side of people being able to find what is important for them, and for what they want to do in their life, and to have flexibility in their course requirements."

The college catalog ends up saying "there are no absolute requirements for the degrees of the college," but the list of expectations of an FPC graduate is extensive, and a recommended four-year schedule looks pretty clearly like a set of requirements.

While students will choose a specific major with its own set of courses, the faculty spend little to no time discussing how an FPC education will help prepare students for careers, the workforce, or otherwise earning a living.

Says Satterfield, "I would think that one of the major functions of education is enjoying your life when you are *not* at a bread-and-butter income-producing task. I guess I believe that a person who gets through an experience something like the Core program and enough accounting and whatever else is required to become a CPA probably has a richer life than the one who becomes a CPA just through learning the technical mastery of moving the figures around in the account books."[53]

Looking back on FPC's founding, Billy Wireman—whose later career as a college president focused on the role of higher education in preparing people for work—believes "the liberal arts, in the minds of many, were seen as almost pristine, academic, intellectual. . . . The humanities had shaped them. And that was, in some substantive degree, true at Florida Presbyterian, and we didn't want to contaminate ourselves with that grubby workplace."

Satterfield recalls of those first planning meetings, "I found myself in a group of alert individuals who seemed well informed in their different disciplines, and who thought beyond their disciplines, and were expressing true concerns about curricular structure. It was the kind of conversation that it was almost impossible to have with more than two or three people at Davidson College. I was inexperienced—I think I wrote Jack that I felt like a pinhead in that group—but I hoped I would have an opportunity to expand what I knew by association with such people."[54]

"We'd fight like dogs in faculty meetings," Keeton remembers, "but it was nothing personal. When the meeting was over, that was it."

Over time it became tradition for science professor Iggy Foster to make a motion to adjourn faculty meetings. The minutes to the meetings, prepared by philosophy professor Keith Irwin, include such conclusions as these:

"All eyes being fastened on Foster, he moved adjournment."

"At 5:20 p.m. the presiding elder in the halls of science suggested that the hour had arrived to move 'out of the ivory palaces into the world of woe,' and so moving, Dr. Foster secured our adjournment."

And "Acting with the speed and penetration of a laser beam, Dr. Foster pierced to the center of everyone's concerns and broke up the meeting with a motion for adjournment which carried unanimously."

Jack Bevan remembers students overhearing a meeting of the faculty during the first year of classes. "Students were working in a nearby office, and they could hear the faculty trouncing each other, faculty members going after each other to the degree that the students became disturbed. They came into my office saying that something must be done because this faculty would blow itself up, that the institution was at a dangerous state with a faculty whose attitudes were so antagonistic to each other. I had to explain to them what development of a curriculum was all about, and that they could be very thankful that they could hear a faculty that was arguing on something important: Curriculum! What they were supposed to learn!"[55]

1.

2.

3.

1. John M. Bevan, Founding Dean of Florida Presbyterian College
2. Hunter Blakely, whose idea it was that a Presbyterian college be established in Florida
3. Jack Bevan and Bill Kadel, Founding Dean and Founding President of Florida
    Presbyterian College

4. Howard Carter, Founding Faculty & Chairman of Division of Humanities
5. John Satterfield, Founding Faculty, Music, with one of his co-presenters at his famous "Myth and Symbol" lecture
6. Robert Meacham, Founding Faculty, Mathematics
7. William C. Wilbur, Founding Faculty, History
8. Clark Bouwman, Founding Faculty, Sociology

9.

10.

11.

12.

9. Kenneth Keeton, Founding Faculty, German
10. I. G. Foster, Founding Faculty, Chairman of Division of Mathematics and Natural Sciences
11. George Reid, Founding Faculty, Biology
12. Pedro Trakas, Spanish, and Fred White, Classics – both Founding Faculty

13.

14.

15.

16.

13. E. Ashby Johnson, Founding Faculty, Religion and Philosophy, and Director of the Western Civilization program
14. Bill Kadel
15. Frances Whitaker, Founding Dean of Women
16. Emma Conboy, President Kadel's secretary

17.

18.

19.

20.

21.

17. Committee of 100 Luncheon for FPC representatives, St. Petersburg (1958, September)
18. Tom West, Director of Admissions
19. President Eisenhower, meeting with William C. Cramer, Bill Kadel, and Phillip Lee in Washington, DC
20. Sterling Watson '69, Peter Meinke Professor of Literature and Creative Writing
21. Groundbreaking, Grover Wrenn and Sara Sue Phelps, founding freshmen

22.

23.

24.

25.

22. Jim Harley, Coach and Athletic Director
23. Peter Meinke, Literature and Creative Writing
24. Cross placed at what became the location of Griffin Chapel; students held chapel services on this open land while still housed on the old campus
25. Groundbreaking ceremony

26.

27.

28.

29.

26. Harry Singletary '68
27. FPC's first Commencement (1964, Pasadena Community Church)
28. Jim Crane, Visual Arts
29. Robert Hodgell, Visual Arts

31.

30.

32.

33.

34.

30. Students' anti-war protest outside Fox Hall
31. James R. Carlson, Theatre
32. President Billy O. Wireman with students
33. Sarah Dean, who joined FPC as Dean of Women in 1968
34. Stephanie Kadel, the author, with her parents, founding freshmen Richard Kadel
    and Karen Reynolds Kadel, and her grandfather, Bill Kadel (Commencement, May 1989)

CHAPTER 7

The Only Way Is Up

Bill Wilbur and I decided this is the last college we want to help give birth to. I suggested sterilization; he preferred a hysterectomy.

Ken Keeton

The day the students arrived on the interim campus of Florida Presbyterian College, Bill Kadel left his office for a while. On that day, for just a moment, he felt he had reached his goals. The campus was ready, the faculty were all there, the first semester of courses was planned. There was nothing for him to do but stand on the sidewalk by the water and watch the founding freshmen unload their belongings, say good-bye to their parents, and find their way to their dorm rooms.

"We have reached and passed the moment of commitment," Kadel wrote that September to college supporters. "We are like an airplane which has started down the runway and has gathered too much speed to stop, and the only way is up. There is nothing as important to us now as the future. It is a future bright with prospect. The real test of our faith and strength is ahead of us. The college is born! Now we must keep it alive."[56]

When the whole student body, faculty, and staff met in the auditorium later for the opening convocation of the college, the anticipation must have been as thick as the humidity outside. As Tom West made his way past the rows of 150-plus students, he knew every one of them by name.

Each student wore a custom-designed lapel pin of a fiddler crab. President Kadel had sent these pins to the founding freshmen the previous spring to welcome them, saying, "You are and always will be someone very special to us." The idea for the pin came from a walking tour of the shoreline of the new campus where thousands of tiny fiddler crabs darted across the sand. "He is a hardy little creature who, when he finds one path blocked, is quick to find another," Kadel wrote to the freshmen in May 1960. "Persistence and patience and courage are attributes we will be looking for in you."[57] Kadel later remembered, "Since we felt that fiddler crabs were the first inhabitants of the land, the first student body might well be called the fiddler crabs."[58] The nickname has persisted to this day.

Bevan and the faculty were equal parts thrilled and exhausted with the start of the first semester. "It was Utopia," Ken Keeton remembers. "I was never happier in my life. And I worked twelve-hour days." One afternoon Keeton and Pedro Trakas were riding in a car with Billy Wireman when they were pulled over for running a Stop sign. "We were talking so much none of us saw it," Keeton says.[59] Wireman remembers seeing fifteen or more faculty cars in the parking lot on the maritime base on Saturday mornings.

"First assembling us as freshmen, administration, staff, and faculty, that young, barrel-chested, red-haired Welshman, Dr. John Bevan stepped to the podium, the masculine eyebrows came down, the eyes flashed like the armor of Achilles, and that massive baritone erupted into, "Who am I? Where am I going?"[60]

So began "Western Civilization and Its Christian Heritage." Bevan gave the first lecture. Each subsequent lecture was given by another professor. It was as much a performance for their colleagues, sitting in the back row, as it was an attempt to teach the students. "People like Howard Carter would nod yes when he agreed and no when he disagreed," remembers art professor Jim Crane (who was hired a couple of years after the founding). "It was horrendously intimidating."

Some lectures looked to shock; others looked for laughs. Ashby Johnson once tore a Bible in half. Another time he claimed the dimensions of Noah's ark would have made the ark sink. Satterfield gave a lecture that included an art slide of *Whistler's Mother*. Before the lecture he had convinced FPC's artist-in-residence, Bob Hodgell, to paint a portrait of FPC's art historian John Dixon as if he were Whistler's mother—his face surrounded by the bonnet and lace. It got big laughs from the crowd but not from Dixon.

The students read and studied like never before. Grover Wrenn remembers, "The opportunity to sit under a palm tree with Dr. Carter and a half-dozen of us in a guided discussion group, talking about Joyce's *Portrait of the Artist as a Young Man* or a Goya painting was a level of challenge and a richness in that kind of interaction that I never experienced in any of the more traditional higher education settings."

Carolyn Hall remembers the work as "very demanding." She got a mid-semester grade of S—but only "by the skin of my teeth." With Bill Wilbur as her assigned professor for the discussion section, her papers came back covered in red ink. "I didn't feel kind of up to what everybody else was doing."

Karen Reynolds (my mother and a founding freshman from St. Petersburg) remembers, "I sat through several lectures always hearing them discussing the symbolism in what we were reading. I didn't know what the word meant, and I didn't even know how to spell it. I was too embarrassed to ask."

For all the challenge to students, the Core course created the learning community Jack Bevan had envisioned. Faculty would pass by groups of students at the pool or in the lounge and hear them talking about *Siddhartha* and Gandhi. Billy Wireman, the coach of the basketball team, reported that his players were discussing the *Iliad* before winning a game against St. Petersburg Junior College.

Creating this learning community around a common course was as much or more of a challenge for the faculty as for the students. "All of us were confronted with materials that many of us had never had to confront before—in a teaching situation certainly—and a lot of them that we had never read before, out of our disciplines," says Wilbur. "And the scientists had the worst time, I think, because they had, of course, the demands of lab time with science courses, and they were very uncomfortable being in a kind of humanities-oriented program. But those who did it learned a lot, too."

"All those who were not either historians or very gifted in literature felt inadequate to it," says Katharine Meacham, wife of math professor Bob. "But they all felt it exciting, and they learned, along with the students, of course. . . . But Bob felt pretty inadequate. He felt adequate in math."

"I couldn't imagine myself teaching Thomas Aquinas for instance," says theatre professor James Carlson. "I'd never read him. I had no background in it. But, you know, I had to find out something. I was as much a learner with relationship to these things as any of the students, and that was a terribly important aspect of what was happening. . . . This was a diverse group, too, and so I was working with science students and literature students and so forth, and sometimes we were all confused."

When the Western Civilization course got to Immanuel Kant's "Prolegomena to Any Future Metaphysics," the faculty blamed Ashby Johnson for urging them to include it. "I can't remember now whether student complaints were as noisy as the faculty's," says Satterfield. "We griped in a Western Civ staff meeting to Ashby, 'Kant is dense, stodgy, turgid, unreadable. Why couldn't he write as plainly as Ben Franklin or Voltaire?' Ashby protested that we were dealing with some of the best insights ever revealed and that we would just have to *think*; that's what Kant did. Fred White then said, 'Ashby, I took the trouble, because the English was so bad, to read the "Prolegomena" in German. It loses something in the original.'"[61]

Faculty also learned together by grading the examinations together. Carlson remembers that he and Johnson were both grading the same students' work. "If we agreed on the grade or evaluation, that was fine. If we didn't, we would have a lengthy discussion. That, you see, was in a sense essential to the Core program that Jack wanted, that it would be a Core for faculty, as well as students."

Jim Crane remembers being "stretched terribly" by his teaching experience in the Core course. The amount of reading he had to keep up with each week, as well as the preparation required for the whole-group lectures he had to give were both "exciting" and "really hard." He says, "You take all the education that I'd had before, and it was absolutely nothing in comparison with working here, as far as what I had to learn, what I had to do, what I learned that I was capable of doing, what I found out I was not capable of doing and all of those things." Crane remembers that another professor said he felt like he owed the college tuition when he left.

"The whole idea of the general education program was a co-learners approach," says Crane. "Bevan would tell us, 'You're a scholar. You know how to organize stuff, you know how to read stuff, so you ought to be able to lead discussions with students on almost any subject. You certainly know as much as most of them.'"

While there were regular meetings of the faculty teaching the course, Crane says they would talk about how to teach the works, but "you were in there with your colleagues, and you didn't want to admit any inadequacies, and so sometimes the most basic questions would never be asked."

Sterling Watson, an FPC graduate, became a professor of creative writing at the college many years after its founding, but his experiences teaching in the Core course echo the stories of the founders. Says Watson,

I had always given lip service to the idea of a community in which people would step outside of their areas of specialization and take the risk of having conversations with young people about works from other areas of specialization, but I had never had the experience. I had been an English teacher before. When I had to teach Plato's *Republic* or Machiavelli's *The Prince*—the list is endless—it was tough. I remember getting up at five in the morning on days when I had to teach. I'd leave the house in the dark with a cup of coffee, a piece of cold toast, and a glass of orange juice, and I'd eat the toast and drink the orange juice on the way to work in my car, and I'd sit in my office for four hours preparing for my class, and I'd go in and teach only marginally well in some cases and come out of there, you know, exhausted and frustrated. The students, in a lot of cases, were not ready for what we were giving them and resisted it pretty mightily. And, you know, there's no person on earth who demands an expert more than an eighteen-year-old freshman.

Watson remembers one of those morning classes when he had to teach the book of Isaiah. He worked hard to make sense of it and even bought the twelve-volume *Interpreter's Bible*. "I had really prepared, and I was just ready as hell to talk about this, and the first question I got was who were the Assyrians? . . . I knew a little about that, but not much, and it just wasn't where I was going to go with that lesson. I just stood there, and what came out of my mouth was a quotation from Byron: 'The Assyrian came down like a wolf on the fold, and his cohorts were gleaming in silver and gold, and the sheen of his spears was like foam on the sea.' And the student just went, 'Yeah, but who were the Assyrians?'"

Watson laughs. "Well, teaching is always risky." He says arguments about the Core course today still highlight a conflict between the value of faculty as generalists and the "idea that students should not be subjected to anything but expertise, that it's fraudulent and damaging to give students teaching that's only barely adequate under the rubric of this idea of community of learners. I suppose both arguments have merit."

He also understands that not all faculty want to make the commitment to becoming a competent generalist. "After three or four years, I really felt like I had gotten a second education. I mean, I felt like I knew something about Western philosophy and Western political thought, and I knew some works of literature very well that I hadn't ever studied, and I had a pretty good grip of the sort of simple story line of the last four-thousand years, and that was a hell of a good feeling to have. But it was paid for with an awful lot of five o'clock in the morning drives with cold toast, and it was paid for with novels that didn't get written. A lot of faculty are just not capable of or able to or willing to do that."

Grover Wrenn's memory of the first years of the college was that students were accepting of the faculty's approach to a shared learning community, finding that it asked more of students by treating them as adults, rather than that it offered less expertise. "It was very much like the message we would say in church, and this was what I heard from the faculty: 'We're all here for the same purpose.' This is a learning community, [as the church] is a worshipping community. We're all on the same journey. Each of us is at a different point on that journey but we're all here to assist each other on that journey. . . . The faculty was saying, 'Look, we've been at this longer than you have. We're here to provide you support and guidance and to facilitate your learning, but in interacting with you, we're going to learn from you.'"

Wrenn continues, "I don't mean that it was a complete laissez-faire attitude, but there was no compulsory class attendance." (At the end of the first year some faculty would complain that students took unfair advantage of that policy and were not in class when they should be.) "And Bevan would not allow gimmicks to be used," says Grover. "I mean, pop quizzes weren't allowed, because that would have made a lie of the freedom to choose where and when you learn. Now, I didn't skip class. Why? Because we had great teachers. . . . It was fun being in most of these classes. I'm not saying every lecture was a John Satterfield special, but by and large this hand-picked faculty were people who lived to teach and to facilitate learning, and it was fun being in their presence. It was just an unusual kind of community, and I think a lot of that richness has continued even until today. I think it's no accident that Eckerd is known for its mentoring relationship between faculty and students. It began that way."

Watson, who came to FPC as a sophomore in 1966, remembers close relations with faculty as well as high expectations:

There was a tendency on the part of the students at that time to build mystiques and mythologies around the faculty. We thought of them as very large. I don't think that we knew much about their actual accomplishments in scholarship, but we thought of them as people to look up to, and, consequently, we wanted to please them and, when we didn't, we felt bad about it. You couldn't come to this place and just sort of hide out and be a C student without standing out. Poor academic performance was tolerated, but it couldn't be winked at.

It was and is the kind of place where people would put pressure on you to be the best that you could be.

They wouldn't accept shoddy work, at least not without identifying it as such, and there was no reluctance about telling someone what they had written was no good or what they turned in was no good. But, at the same time, there wasn't a sense of absolute disastrous consequences. The college welcomed underachievers, and it was the place of the tenth last chance, you know. Now that I know how places like this work, I think part of that was because we just probably couldn't afford to kick students out right and left. We had to try to keep them, and so consequently we kept some we shouldn't have kept and we saved some. And I suppose you could say I was one who was saved.

Just as the founding freshmen were given academic freedom and therefore responsibility for their own learning, they were also free to create the social scene of this new institution—and therefore had to shoulder responsibility for defining student life at FPC. "We imbibed the heady brew of the 'break with tradition,' the 'new start,' and 'building (or founding) a college,'" writes founding freshman Paul Hoffman. "In our naïveté we came to believe that there was little we could not do."[62] In their first weeks, a group of students sat up one night creating a class flag featuring the fiddler crab. The next day it was hoisted up the flag pole to cheers from the whole student body.

"There were no traditions," Wrenn remembers. "There was no student government. There was no student newspaper. All these things had to be created, and there were enough jobs to go around that everybody could have multiple roles." Grover was elected the first chief justice of the honor court. He helped write the honor code (to which trustees asked students not to take an oath "because such oaths are dangerous and because the Honor Code is considered a part of the way of life of the college").[63] He also took photographs for the student paper, the *Trident*.

Decisions were quickly made to distinguish FPC from other colleges. Fraternities and sororities were out. Basketball was in; football was out; intramural athletics were in. A marching band and school song were out; a large, touring choir was in. Themed dances became a favorite social event on a campus with few amenities for students. The first was the impromptu "Hurricane Hop" to coincide with the arrival of Hurricane Donna in September 1960 (which canceled classes but caused no damage). Picnics and cookouts brought students together with faculty and their families.

So did the basketball team—an unexpected force for school spirit that first year. The administration of the college had decided early on that athletics would not be subsidized, so when Wireman came in as associate director of physical education, his plans focused more on the required physical education courses, not on coaching. But, he says, "I remember looking out one day and seeing some students practicing basketball. And, my goodness, three or four of them could flat play. They came to me and said, 'Why don't we have a team?' And I said, in the spirit of the college, 'Why not?'"[64]

The team practiced outdoors and hosted games in a neighborhood youth center gymnasium. Their first game was against the University of South Florida, which had also just opened its doors in 1960. Says Wireman, "It is still debatable as to whether they were a team or whether we were a team, but nonetheless we took credit for the win." Much of the FPC community turned out to cheer on their "Tritons." (In

November 1960 students voted that the FPC mascot would be the Triton, a sea god from Greek mythology who had the torso of a man and tail of a fish and calmed waves with his conch-shell trumpet.)[65] After the game Kadel made his way over to Wireman. "I thought he was going to say, 'Billy, congratulations on the win.' What he said was, 'Who pays for the referees?'"

While the students were building their own traditions, the wives of the faculty were also making their own distinctive decisions. That first semester they had an official meeting at Louise Bevan's house. "We wrote up a list of things we will not be asked to do," says Katharine Meacham. "Each woman is to do and to be as she chooses. We will set our own roles. We will not bake cookies, fry chicken, etc. Nor should anyone feel compelled to join this group."[66] They did start a book club together, but they all led busy lives outside of the college. Many of the women worked in the community as teachers and artists and dedicated volunteers. They entertained students in their homes as they desired, and those students still treasure the memories of getting to know the faculty's spouses, children, and pets and being included in engaging conversations.

In the later 1960s Sterling Watson developed that kind of relationship with theatre professor Jim Carlson. "I think he is the smartest man I've ever known," says Watson. "I think he has probably the best mind I've ever encountered. He was legendary, especially among the people who eventually socialized with him, as I did." Watson describes gatherings at Carlson's house of several professors and as many as ten or fifteen juniors and seniors, along with great food, a lot of drinking, and intellectual conversations that were not "pretentious or heavy" and often turned political. "Those were really great times," Watson remembers. "I mean, if I could think of a time in my life when I was a part of what could really be called an intellectual community with an artistic community with real values and goals and a high level of discourse, that would be it."

Although cars on campus were prohibited from the start, most college policies for student behavior were created as the need arose. Tom West, as dean of men, worked closely with the dean of women, Frances Whitaker. He remembers, "Many times we would be walking down the hall and say, 'Oh, we don't have a policy on that, do we? 'Well, here's what it is.' And when we got to the desk, we'd type it, and it was a policy."

One of those policies was that a sailboat that had been given to the college could not be taken out by students without a faculty member on board. This came about after some students had borrowed it and not taken very good care of it. But then, as West remembers it, Ashby Johnson, Bob Meacham, and another one or two professors went sailing and got stuck on a sandbar and had to be pulled off by the Coast Guard. "The next day," West remembers, "in a special edition of the student newspaper was this new policy: No faculty can take the sailboat out without a student being on board."

As fellow deans of students, Whitaker was more strict and West was more permissive, and they often did not agree. One time West wanted to turn some old, walk-in freezers off the student lounge into "dating rooms" where students could have a little privacy. Whitaker worried, "They'll be in there doing things they should not be doing." The compromise was to remove the doors so students could use them, but they could still be seen.

Another disagreement arose over the arrival of a British submarine in the marina. West saw it as a great opportunity for cross-cultural contact; Whitaker worried about the young women getting involved with British sailors. She locked the dormitory doors at night until the submarine had left. West says Whitaker mellowed over time. West's feeling was, "I had met all these students and their families and knew them as people, and I wanted them to have a wonderful, free experience of learning how to be on their own."

Dealing with the students' antics was not always so wonderful, however. West remembers getting called by the night watchman at three o'clock in the morning because the young men were having a water fight. "Well, I dragged myself out of bed, came over as the dean of men, stood in front of the barracks, drew myself to my full stature, and said, 'This has got to stop!' And, at that moment, a balloon full of water came sailing down and hit me. It couldn't have been better if it had been the Three Stooges—it just hit me and splattered all over. And there were screams of laughter, and I just turned right around, got in my car, and went back home. That was the end of my stopping of water fights. . . . I think that was one of the reasons why I decided to be the director of counseling rather than dean of men."

Another student incident that first year was less humorous. On a sunny afternoon, between two wings of the men's dorm, some students were hitting plastic golf balls with a golf club when a stray cat wandered through. As Wrenn remembers hearing about it, "They started chasing the cat, and it wound up that one of the students swung the golf club and hit the cat and badly injured it." The cat ended up being put to sleep. At least one professor became enraged over this act, and the issue was brought before the brand-new honor court. "We held that the honor code didn't relate to this conduct," says Wrenn. "The conduct was not very noble, but it did not constitute a violation of the honor code."

The issue sparked debate among the faculty and administration about whether the student should be dismissed (he was not) and whether the college was too lax about student behavior. "There was a fair amount of controversy on campus," says Wrenn, "enough that Bevan called me in to account for the honor court, and I did. He didn't grill me, he didn't put me on the defensive terribly, but he didn't signal what his view was. After I'd articulated the reasoning that the court had used, he looked at me and he said, 'I'm completely comfortable with what you have said, and when some of my academic colleagues show a greater measure of concern for improving the quality of humankind, I may join them in their concern for other parts in the animal kingdom.'"

FPC was now a college in action, no longer a theoretical vision of a Utopian learning community. And like any institution of higher education, it would continue to be challenged by the behaviors of its students—and its board and faculty and staff.

Some students were rule followers; others were making their own rules. Carolyn Hall became treasurer of the Student Christian Association, and she remembers being teased by certain male students as being part of the "God Squad." She says women students all wore dresses to class, and while she had a different date for every dance and social event, she was not aware of students sleeping together or using drugs. A bus came to campus on Sunday mornings to drive her and other students to Pasadena Community Church.

Another student, possibly from the backwoods of north Florida or Alabama, was secretly dubbed "Swamp Girl" by some faculty when she tried to use her sexy wiles to improve her grades. When she was having trouble with math, she sidled up to Bob Meacham and said, "Dr. Meacham, are you ever over here at night?"

"No, *ma'am*," he said.

Later she met with Billy Wireman about her grade in physical education. He remembers she rubbed a pencil up and down his arm and said something like, "I sure have enjoyed your class, Dr. Wireman. I hope you've enjoyed me, too."

Meanwhile, Grover Wrenn was dating a fellow freshman from his hometown, and by the end of their first year she was pregnant. They decided to get married, and Jack Bevan counseled them to make sure they were prepared for this commitment. The students needed to marry quickly before the next school year began, so Bevan arranged for a friend of his, a Presbyterian minister in Georgia, to marry them. He even loaned them his station wagon to drive to Georgia. Bevan met with Grover's parents "and vouched for me," says Wrenn. With Grover's parents no longer financially responsible for him, Bevan activated Grover's need-based scholarship and worked through a budget with him. Wrenn still gets choked up when he tells this story, remembering all that Jack did for him and his young family.

As students progressed through the first year at FPC—with the building of the new campus moving slowly, the demands of their classes weighing them down, and their new identities in flux—the "heady brew" of a new start occasionally tasted bitter. Not all the students were excelling academically. Eleven dropped out before the end of the first semester, only 20 percent passed all their courses that first term, and thirty-four students received letters during the holiday break suggesting they not come back.[67]

Those who remained knew their studies would have to come first, even over helping to create the college's traditions. "It was easy to pick at little things," Hoffman says. "We wanted so badly for OUR college to be perfect. In our idealism we denied our own humanity and tried to deprive our mentors of theirs. . . . Elections for new officers showed how little of the old founding spirit was left. The *Trident* spoke of 'wide-spread apathy.'"

Hoffman's take on this situation (as he wrote in 1964) was that the students were "choosing our academic careers and shirking our community responsibility. . . . FPC, very likely, was not going to have the customs and institutions . . . that some persons had envisioned here. . . . We were forgetting that a new academic scheme was not likely to produce or tolerate traditional patterns of college life."

He says Kadel "asked the students to show a more positive attitude: 'Look back on our short history and see what has been done. Then look to the future with confidence and faith. We have established a goal for ourselves and we will achieve it.'"[68]

Students, faculty, and administration alike watched eagerly that second semester for weekly notices on how many new students had decided to attend FPC in the fall of 1961.

January 1961 brought relief from the wilting heat and one of FPC's most notable contributions to the history of American higher education—the one-month interim term, now known as winter term. "I suspect three or four hundred colleges have it now," says Billy Wireman. "At the time, everyone said, 'Oh my gosh, January in St. Petersburg. They'll be at the beach, they'll be in Ft. Lauderdale.' And the truth of the matter is that library circulation increased during January."

Indeed, winter term was an unqualified success in FPC's curriculum, whether as a time for experimental group projects, independent study, or international travel. Early on, one student spent the month in New Orleans working on a politician's campaign. Another group built a harpsichord. Some theatre students directed their own play; others learned tai chi. An art student built a potter's wheel and taught himself to throw clay; another set up a darkroom in one of the campus bathrooms. Wrenn undertook chemistry-related research projects during winter term that he says "equaled anything I did in graduate school, in terms of complexity and the discipline that I was taught."

Over the years professors capitalized on the opportunity to design short, creative courses. Keeton taught students to speak Icelandic one year and had a group design their own religion another year. He also taught a winter term German class using a technique known as "superlearning," which involved repeating the new material in three different voices while playing baroque music. "Strangely enough," says Keeton, "when you finished that, the students knew it. It had gone into their minds."

My own winter term courses in the 1980s are some of the most memorable classes I took at Eckerd. Those included a study of Howard Gardner's "multiple intelligences" through the reading of biographies, and a review of the history of filmmaking—taught by two philosophy professors—which introduced me to classic movies I'd never seen before.

The success of independent study in the winter term encouraged more student-designed independent study during the regular semesters. It also led to the design of "directed study" courses—a syllabus of readings and assignments created by a professor that a student would undertake on his or her own, with occasional meetings with the professor.

Perhaps the most important result of the 4-1-4 schedule, however, was the opportunity for international travel. In the second year of the college, in January 1962, Clark Bouwman (sociology) and Pedro Trakas (Spanish) took a group of FPC students out of the country—to a Mexican village to study the language and culture of the area. About thirty students participated. They stayed in a YMCA camp a mile outside the village center, slept in tents, cooked their own meals, hiked in the mountains, and spent time with the residents. "It was all just a joy," Bouwman remembers.

In 1964 Bill Wilbur joined other professors in taking a group of students to London, where they studied English history. Wilbur's history majors were able to access primary sources at city hall and prestigious London libraries.

Carolyn Hall was on that trip to London. It was her senior year. She was a French major and spent much of the time studying for her comprehensive exams at the University of London Library, but she still made time for the tours, plays, and museum visits.

Bouwman quickly became the college's best resource for planning these trips. "Bouwman was a genius at getting things set up," says Wilbur, "and it would cost as little as possible and yet come off as a good program." Before long Bouwman was relieved of his classroom duties and put in charge of international study and independent study. In 1970 he negotiated the lease of a 200-year-old Georgian row house in London to house students and faculty on semester-long trips to England. The "London Study Centre" has remained a central piece of the college's international program ever since.

In the summer of 1963 Keeton took a group of forty students to Germany for two months. It was the first of many trips he would make with FPC students back to the country where he had served in the war and first fell in love with the language and culture. He wanted the experience to help students "recognize that people are basically the same, and cultures vary, obviously. . . I've always thought that the best approach to learning is comparative. . . . Students can see these things with their own eyes; they don't have to read about it in the book. And they have discussions about these things when they're abroad." Keeton later extended his interest in international experiences to encourage exchange programs between German and American college students and to bring German natives to FPC as teaching assistants.

Back on campus the various disciplines of the college were beginning to find their own ways. Despite all the talk of minimal departmental divisions and interdisciplinary learning, despite all the time and energy spent in the Core course, students were also choosing majors, and faculty were teaching the courses they knew best.

Keeton and fellow language professor Trakas designed, marketed, administered, and taught a foreign language immersion program during the summer of 1961. Students came from all over the country, lived on the campus, and pledged not to speak English for six weeks. Bevan agreed to let the professors create the program as long as they took care of all the tasks involved. It was indicative of Bevan's supportive oversight of the faculty. "He had an incredible ability to push himself out of anybody's way," says Satterfield. "He would say, 'If you want to do it and you think it's good, I trust your judgment and I support you.' That was all you got from him, all the time."

Grover Wrenn remembers taking German from Keeton. Wrenn had a pronounced southern drawl that made his German pronunciation rather interesting. Keeton started to laugh and said, "Mr. Wrenn, there are no such sounds in the German language. This is going to be a challenge for both of us."

Carolyn Hall took finite math from Meacham. "He was all over the blackboard," she remembers. "It was the most amazing thing. I just held on by my fingertips."

When he began to offer sociology courses in the second year, Bouwman's classes were packed with twenty-five to thirty students, and sociology became one of the most popular majors.

Students also flocked to Jack Bevan's and Tom West's psychology courses. Starting with an introductory course, the discipline gradually added experimental psychology, personality theory, and other courses as the semesters progressed. West also learned more about counseling from his senior colleague: "When I first came here, I was a crew cut psychologist," says West. "A student would come in, and I'd analyze that student's problem before he or she sat down and then would tell the student what to do. And I remember Jack Bevan saying, 'You just need to remember that they need to talk to you.'"

In the third year all juniors were required to take a core course in Asian studies. The requirement lasted for several more years, but by all accounts it was one of the few academic experiments that did not succeed. "Most of us were totally lost in that course," remembers Hall.

In connection with the course, FPC joined three other Florida liberal arts colleges in hosting a conference on Southeast Asia, funded by the Danforth Foundation. Paul Hoffman later wrote, "One of the speakers had gotten the impression that we were a small and not very spectacular institution. He hadn't really prepared, he said. When he got here and was cross-examined by some of us, he realized his mistake and apologized to the heads of the conference."[69]

Word was getting out that impressive things were happening in that little college in St. Pete. Each new class of freshmen was bigger than the one before (total enrollment increased from 151 to over 1000 in the first decade), and public interest in the college's efforts was high. Billy Wireman, who branched out from athletics to college development, was as impressed as anyone by what was taking place on the old maritime base, and he took a message of naïve optimism to the public. "We were going to save the world," he remembers. "I mean, we were going to save it by noon tomorrow, and there was just no turning back."

CHAPTER 8

A Lively Encounter with Christianity

We wanted to be the best small, church-related liberal arts college in the country, and we thought we were.

Katharine Meacham

Classics professor Fred White used to claim that when he went in to interview with Bill Kadel for a faculty position at Florida Presbyterian College, Kadel asked him, "Do you believe in the Virgin birth?"

Fred answered, "Yes, sir. I believe there are virgins born every day."

No one really believes Fred said that. But this "Kadel test" to determine a potential faculty member's commitment to evangelical Christianity has become a treasured, though possibly apocryphal, story in FPC history. While many people claim that his most common religious question in interviews was indeed "Do you believe in the Virgin birth?" most faculty members' own recollections are that they personally did not get asked that question.

Iggy Foster, the physicist, does not remember talking theology at all with Kadel but only checking to make sure there would be no rules against faculty drinking alcohol. While Kadel was an avowed teetotaler, he assured Foster that "I might discourage big gatherings where drinking was involved, but what you do in your own home is up to you."[70]

Ken Keeton was not questioned either. He says, "I think my reputation preceded me. I had been very active at Wake Forest, and I had been a Sunday school superintendent. I immediately joined a Presbyterian church here in St. Pete, became active in that, and sang in the choir."

However he inquired about a potential faculty member's religious commitment, it certainly did matter to Kadel what the professors believed. Bevan was charged with recruiting a Christian faculty, and Kadel had an opportunity to review Bevan's choices. "All of them had to indicate that they were sympathetic and understanding and accepted the Christian faith," Tom West remembers, "and the president was the one who was in charge of asking them questions along that line. And they all passed."

In later years founding faculty would warn new recruits of Kadel's demanding interview. Jim Crane, who became an art professor at FPC in 1963, says, "I was warned he was going to ask, 'Do you believe in the Virgin birth?' And I was thinking how I was going to answer that. But Kadel came in, and he said, 'It's just remarkable. You look just like my minister back when I was a boy.' So he talked to me about his minister that I looked like, and we had a really good talk, but he never asked me about the Virgin birth."

Poet Peter Meinke's visit to campus in 1966 to be considered for a position as a literature and creative writing professor has become the stuff of legend. He already knew some of the faculty at FPC, including theatre professor Jim Carlson. They wanted him to join them at FPC, but they also knew he was not a

116

churchgoing man. When they told him about Kadel's interview questions, Meinke remembers, "everybody was afraid I would just flunk this cold. They were very nervous for me." Carlson got the idea to volunteer to do the chapel service in advance of Meinke's visit (faculty rotated responsibility for chapel services) and to have students read Meinke's poetry. "They read every one of my poems that was at all vaguely spiritual, of which I have quite a few, I must say." So when he went in to interview with Dr. Kadel later, Meinke remembers, "He got up and he shook my hand. He said, 'It's so good to have a Christian poet on campus.' And I said, 'Thank you, sir.'"

The ruse almost backfired, however, later that day at lunch when, among a table full of professors, Kadel asked Meinke to say the blessing. "Seconds pass as large as minutes," writes fellow writing professor Sterling Watson in a retirement tribute to Meinke almost thirty years later.

The room is silent. Meinke opens one eye and sees, nearby, a professor with his eyes thoughtfully closed, nearby another with thumb and forefinger prayerfully pressed to forehead. Meinke moves his head a few degrees to the right and spies President Kadel at the head of the table. The great man's eyes are closed, but is that the quiver of a question at the corner of his mouth? Is he about to say something?

Lo! Someone speaks. It is a professor to whom Peter Meinke is destined to be forever grateful. A man to whom Meinke owes his job, and to whom you and I owe the history we share with Peter Meinke as colleague and friend. It is Keith Irwin who speaks.

"Thank you for that fine Quaker blessing, Dr. Meinke."
President Kadel looks at Meinke for a long moment, then
says, "Ah-men," and the good professors sit down to eat.[71]

For all their warnings to each other the early faculty were
mostly all personally committed to the Christian faith and to
discovering its role in higher education. In a May 1960 report to
the Presbyterian Synod, the newly hired professors are described
as "a faculty of deep Christian convictions. They are men and
women of conscience, challenged by the concept of the
curriculum, inspired by what this college will become in the
years ahead. They are men and women of faith, yet it is the faith
of the inquiring mind. They are persons of ideals *and* ideas."[72]

Keeton says the fact that FPC was church-related was very
important to him. "I had spent all my life in church, and I knew
that the basic premise, the Christian principles, were right. . . .
I thought of all the good things that a Christian college meant,
and, to me, the Christian principles are admirable. . . .
Christianity is a noble religion, and once we established that the
college would be open to anybody, then the Christian principle
really flowed here."

Jim Carlson came to FPC in 1964 partly because of its
church affiliation. "I was very much interested in religious
aspects of theatre, and I had participated in some organizations
of that kind and attended some conferences, national and
international. I was editing a magazine called *Religious Theater*,
and we published it for a couple of years after I was down here."

West remembers the college administration praising his
involvement in a local church. "When I became a deacon of the

First Presbyterian Church, I got a letter from President Kadel, saying, 'Oh, how wonderful.' Then when I became an elder, I got another one, and then I began doing preaching. He loved things like that."

Despite their own commitments to Christianity, the faculty certainly saw that Kadel's role not only as president but also as the direct representative and liaison to the Presbyterian Church and the board of trustees (which were essentially one and the same in the early years) gave him a different set of priorities than the faculty—priorities the faculty sometimes had to work around to accomplish their academic goals. It was a familiar strain between professors and administrators in higher education, but the situation was both less intense and more complicated during FPC's beginnings.

It was less intense because the college was so small and so new. Everyone had a hands-on role in making things work, nothing was set in stone to be preserved "like we've always done it," and Kadel gave considerable freedom to Bevan and the faculty to create the college as they wanted it to be. Tom West remembers, "He was the kind of person who could say to Jack Bevan, 'This is your area. I'm going to connect with churches. I'm going out there and see if we can find the finances to make this college work. I'm going to be the inspiration. I'm going to be the one that brings the influence of God into this. Jack, you find the faculty, you develop the curriculum. Tom, you look at the students. And we'll all work together, but we all have our thing that we have to do.'"

Billy Wireman, the college's second president, also remembers that division of labor. "That college would not have raised that kind of money if people hadn't believed in Kadel. Bevan was the inside guy to put the academic vision together, but I saw the absolute critical part that Bill Kadel was playing in the college, and I don't mind telling you I was worried when I took over whether I could continue that or not."

The president's relationship with the faculty was also perhaps more complicated than in most college settings, because the college was started by religious men who were not academic scholars, who then intentionally set out to recruit faculty who would question tradition and think critically about everything, including religion. Says John Satterfield, "While Bill Kadel had great energy and a very wonderful ability to assimilate, very quickly, what he heard academicians say, and he could paraphrase what they said in ways that were not offensive to them when he made speeches to various publics, it was also clear about Bill Kadel that he was not the intellectual leader—academic, in the usual sense—that Jack Bevan was."[73]

Bill and Kay Kadel also readily admit that they did not connect well socially with the faculty. They bought a home far away from where the faculty lived, and Kay did not do things with the wives of faculty members. She remembers being shocked the first time she and Bill were invited to a cocktail party. "People don't invite ministers to cocktail parties, but they do college presidents," she told a reporter for the *St. Petersburg Times*. "I was a little embarrassed."[74] The Kadels attended the more staid First Presbyterian Church, while many of the faculty attended the more liberal and folksy Lakeview Presbyterian Church.

Billy Wireman remembers that when he came to interview with Kadel for a founding position as director of physical education, Kadel was "quite interested in my religious underpinnings."

He asked me if I was a believer, and I said, "Yes, sir, I am."

And he said, "Well, what does it mean to you?"

And I said, "Well, I try to shape my life based on my religious understandings."

And he said, "Are you doing it?"

"Well, I hope so."

"Well, how will you know?"

It was very, very penetrating. He was smart. It was a grilling, an intensive grilling, and finally he said to me, "Do you think that we can combine a strong intellectual academic component with the church?"

And I said, "Of course." I was a graduate of Georgetown in Kentucky, which is a Baptist college, and so I saw firsthand a way that a college can be at once Christian and, at the same time, academic.

Bill was very interested in that, and he made a confession to me that I have not forgotten to this day because it shows you what kind of humility he had and a sense that he was still a learner himself. He said, "Well, I have to learn about that because, you know, I'm coming from an explicitly religious pastoral background, and my work has been mostly in nurturing, proclaiming. And I have to learn about that, but I can do it." And there was no doubt that he could do it.

What did it mean to be a Christian college, a church-related college, a community of intellect and of faith? It was a question that Kadel and Bevan and the rest of the college community would ask many times in the early years and forever afterward. FPC decided right away that it would not be a pre-seminary school, that it would not require chapel attendance or Bible classes, and that it would not indoctrinate students. But the founders had a harder time articulating what the college *would* do to combine a foundation in the Christian faith with a strong academic experience.

Jack Bevan struggles with these questions in a paper he wrote titled "Betwixt and Between,"[75] which refers both to the Christian college's place between the church and the secular world and the college student's place between childhood and adulthood. "We are dealing with young people who are restless and confused," Bevan writes. "Confused because they are interested not only in 'competence' but in ethical, moral and religious standards, in a personal and national ethic and morality, in a purpose in being. . . . The young person today lives more precariously between the realms of dogma and skepticism and with a sense of *urgency* asks the questions, 'Who am I?' 'What am I' 'Where am I going' 'Where are we going?' In essence, his question is 'What can I believe?'—since what he believes is the primary reference point in defining who he is and the ethical judgments he will make."

Bevan discusses the challenge of helping students answer these questions in most college and university settings, where the focus is on "knowing how to do and to know" but not "how to be." He notes that it is much harder for a college to measure whether students have developed "concern" than whether they have gained competence in a field of study, so most colleges don't pursue the former goal. But if a college wants to help students develop both competence and concern, to discover their own convictions, which they can "defend critically and live with emotionally," the student "must have the opportunity to explore critically all ideas and positions of thought, not merely those which we hope he might espouse."

A church-related institution, Bevan says, has advantages over other colleges in this pursuit: "The first assumption is the acknowledgment that all truth is of God. Confident in this assumption, the Christian college can be fearless in its exploration, free to gather, refine and pass on the many facets of truth. . . . Secondly, it operates on the assumption that the Church has created the college so that it might truly be in the world for the world, just as the Servant Lord himself was in the world for the world. . . . In this sense the college can be unrelenting in its search for relevance."

Bevan goes on to say that the church-related college, in affirming a role as servant, can exhort students to express concern for and serve others and that while many idols vie for a student's loyalty, the church-related college makes sure "that the Christian faith will be given a forthright hearing."

It was these assumptions, these roles for the college, these goals for the student, that defined Bevan's image of a Christian college, that influenced the kind of curriculum and educational philosophy he brought to FPC, and that permeated the classroom experiences of students and faculty.

Satterfield's memory of the teaching at FPC was that professors were able to teach the Bible and some theology and "frequently succeeded in getting students concerned with problems of value and even religious values with minimum indoctrination in religion." He suspects "there was a good bit of implicit political indoctrination." He further recalls, "I did do some visiting teaching at the University of Texas one summer and found professors there much more frightened about making any statement at all about religion or about politics than I was at Florida Presbyterian College. I think that the institution was marvelously free."[76]

"I think the words 'a lively encounter with Christianity' are what we used," says West. "I thought it needed to be encountered, so that students would understand the Christian message and journey of the Christian in this world, but it should not in any way be made compulsory. So we did have the Christian heritage brought in with the Core program. We did have the chapel. We did have a chaplain. But in no way was it a compulsory experience. And I think it worked well, I really do."

Grover Wrenn, who came as a founding freshman, became active in the campus ministry that students organized. "But I'm not sure," he says, "that was as important to me as the role models that so many of the faculty represented. . . . Their faith commitment was manifest in the way they acted out their lives and in their conversations, and it was just another enriching part of the community."

Sterling Watson feels that "the college has never, at any point in its history, in its classrooms done anything but the very best job of handling religious subject matter, in my view. It's always been handled in a fashion that was true to principles of scholarship and inquiry and critical thinking, but also in a fashion that honored notions of faith and mystery."

Part of being true to principles of scholarship meant challenging students to think critically about what they had learned to believe as children. Bill Wilbur echoes the intent of many faculty when he says the college should "give an opportunity for people to go beyond a Sunday school understanding of what religion is and what Christianity is."

West remembers many of the students he recruited to FPC were from Christian backgrounds but were saying, "I don't want this being pushed down my throat anymore. Thank you for letting me now do some thinking." But he also remembers the faculty could push the students out of their comfort zone. "We had faculty who felt it was very important to make these students think deeply, to confront them seriously with their 'Jesus loves me, this I know, for the Bible tells me so' . . . naïveté about their religion."

Karen Reynolds, a founding freshman who grew up in the Methodist church, was in Clark Bouwman's discussion group for Western Civilization. She remembers, "One of the very first assignments we were given was to write our understanding of original sin and defend it. I did what I thought was a pretty decent job. But when I got it back, he had written on my paper, 'You can't rely on your Sunday school upbringing anymore. You have to learn to think for yourself.' My parents saw that and they were in an uproar."

West remembers students would "come to me in tears and say, 'I don't know what to do. I don't know what to believe.' And they would go home at Christmas and tell their parents what was going on, and their parents would just raise Cain."

Minutes from a March 1962 faculty meeting include this statement: "President Kadel encouraged the faculty to respond sympathetically to student needs when students feel that their faith is being questioned."

West, who left admissions and became director of counseling at FPC in 1961, remembers helping students with this crisis of faith:

> I would tell them I have my doubts, too, and I can understand that there would be in you some confusion, because I came up through the Presbyterian Sunday school programs just like you. And I remember going to Davidson and having my first professor of Bible I, a fellow named Everhard, come in the room, take the Bible, put it on the floor and step on it and say, 'This is not holy.'. . . I had my shocks about this, too, and finally realized that it's to my advantage to understand that there are different ways of looking at religion, looking at the Christian faith, looking at God, and other people can have their beliefs, too, and I'm not going to be one that says mine is the only way and, if you shatter mine, then I'm just a basket case. A lot of them just needed to talk about it.

West also cautioned other faculty that they needed to help students through this time of questioning. He found that some colleagues would tear down students' belief systems in class but, when asked later for help, would answer, "You've got to figure this out for yourself." West told them, "You've got to share with the students where you are in your beliefs." Tom feels this was the beginning of the college's mentoring program, an approach to faculty-student relations that continues to this day. Faculty mentors go beyond academic advising to talk with students about various topics in their lives, their families, their worries and fears, and their futures.

The result for students of challenging and questioning religious beliefs was not always a "closer walk with Thee." Wrenn admits that "part of my reaction to the part of my life that I spent at FPC was to become cynical about the institutional church. . . . I had become self-righteously indignant about the frailties and the hypocrisy of the institutional church. Part of it was the racial foment of that period and the fact that eleven a.m. on Sunday morning was the most segregated hour of the week in America. I thought I didn't need the church. . . . My reaction was to absent myself from it for twenty years, which was to my detriment and that of my kids."

While they did not know about Grover's particular choices, the potential for this kind of reaction to FPC's approach to a lively encounter with religion was surely a concern of Presbyterians who supported the college but expected it to result in pillars of the church, not morally driven rebels. This conflict came to a head more than once in the development of the college as faculty became public activists for social justice and students became poster children for the sixties counterculture.

CHAPTER 9

A Bitter Pill

But we stand in life at midnight, we are always on the threshold of a new dawn.

Martin Luther King Jr.

The Board of Trustees of Florida Presbyterian College came to St. Petersburg in May 1962 to discuss a variety of matters. No doubt they took a tour of the campus construction underway in south St. Pete. Back in a meeting room on the interim campus, they surely reviewed the budget and major gifts and financial projections. They probably heard reports about new hires, library acquisitions, student achievement, and the basketball team's wins and losses.

By that point some of the thirty suit-and-tie, white businessmen in that room were probably getting sleepy. The college had been up and running for two full academic years now, and while much was still required to build the campus and fund operations, the excitement of the founding years had given way to orderly agendas and predictable updates.

Then President Kadel turned to the report of entering students for the 1962–63 school year. He quoted statistics on the number of applicants, the percentage accepted and rejected, and the number of deposits the college had received from those planning to enroll. And, perhaps as casually as possible, he mentioned that the college could enroll its first black student that fall, a rising junior transfer student from Gibbs Junior College.

Gibbs was an all-black college in St. Petersburg. The applicant, Howard Eugene Kennedy, had been attending a Sunday night discussion group of FPC and Gibbs students at Ken Keeton's home. He was encouraged by Keeton and other faculty to apply.

Kadel hoped it would be treated as just another report item, but he knew better. He had been in those meetings between the Northern and Southern Presbyterian churches where the issue of accepting black students had caused such rancor. He knew the trustees did not all agree and that the issue had simply been set aside, like a neglected crack in the foundation that could eventually bring the building down.

Philip Lee, chairman of the board, says that Kadel "recognized that he had a real problem in dealing with people like myself. . . . I was from the black belt of Alabama, and I just felt there was a barrier there that was intended from on high that we shouldn't be trying to pull them in [to be] a part of this undertaking."[77]

The board erupted in heated conversation. Lee resigned as chairman, and trustee Colin English (president of First Securities Company of Florida in Tallahassee) agreed to take the chairmanship of the board for a year. The board voted sixteen to thirteen not to accept Kennedy. Their official position was that the college could not accept black students while housed on city property and that the board would reconsider the issue after moving to the new campus in the fall.

"While the meeting of the board was going on," Kadel remembers, "word leaked out that the vote had been taken and the young man had been denied admission. By the time the board meeting was concluded, the faculty was already in session. I was asked to meet with them, at which time they asked me to submit my resignation. I had indicated to the faculty earlier on that if the college were to be a segregated college I would not be its president. To the faculty this meant that now was the time for me to fulfill that commitment. It was my judgment, however, that we would be able to resolve this matter in a favorable way, given some time, and therefore I refused to submit my resignation."

Jack Bevan remembers, "What came out of that board meeting was an unbelievable thing: 'Not at this time!' . . . The faculty came there knowing that in some institutions in the South, even church institutions, there was still a 'not at this time' kind of thing, but it wouldn't be here at FPC. Some of them wouldn't have come if there were any question about that. I wouldn't have."[78]

Bob Meacham, the mathematics professor, came home that day, sat down on the bench at his front door, and wept. "This was our dream," his wife, Katharine, remembers. "We'd just poured so much into it, and if we were going to be Christian and do the right thing, honest to Pete, of course we had to accept that student. It was heartrending."

Clark Bouwman, professor of sociology, remembers that Kadel had told the faculty early on that, during the hiring process, every one of them had asked him individually where the college stood on the race issue, and his response was always that FPC was not going to exclude blacks.

"I think many of us felt that Bill could have taken a stronger role at the beginning," says Bouwman, "in saying to the trustees before the school began, 'Look, I know what the customs of the South have been, but we cannot do that. We're an innovative, new learning institution, and we must not fall into the old practices.'"

Ashby Johnson felt "huge resentment" toward Kadel and considered him "about as low as a college president could be."[79]

John Satterfield called it a "bitter pill to swallow," saying "I never regained the no-reservations trust that I earlier had in the institution."[80]

The faculty held an AAUP meeting—an official gathering under the auspices of the American Association of University Professors—to discuss the matter without Kadel present. They voted unanimously on May 25 to empower the president to "inform the Board, at his discretion, of the conviction of the faculty that it cannot serve in a segregated college."[81]

When Kadel saw them exiting the meeting, he commented, "So that's what being in AAUP means—you can have a meeting without the president."

When the faculty met on the evening of the board meeting, Lowell Brandle, a reporter from the *St. Petersburg Times* who had covered the college's founding from the beginning, was there. Kadel recalls what happened next:

At ten o'clock that night I got a call from Lowell asking me to meet him. I met him at my office, and he read me a release he had prepared to be sent out over the national network of communications. When he had read the statement he said to me, "What is your reaction to this?"

My comment was, "Lowell, you have the ethics of your profession to guide you, and I would not ask you not to send that out. I would say to you that in my judgment, if this issue becomes a public issue, I think that the ability of the college to sustain itself in these very early days would be very difficult."

He looked at me and said, "You don't mind standing alone do you?"

My comment to his was, "I wish I had a lot of people standing with me, but I came here to help build a college and I'm not about to give up now."

Lowell tore up that paper—a very significant event in the history of the college.

While the press was keeping it quiet, the faculty were taking a stand. On May 31 they met with Kadel, who, according to the faculty meeting minutes, "invited members of the faculty to give him evidence that an emergency situation exists so that he could call a special meeting of the Board to reconsider its action. An emergency would exist, in the President's judgment, if he were presented during the afternoon with a number of resignations from the faculty, resignations stemming from the Board's action."[82]

He got them.

All but two members of the faculty resigned. Jack Bevan placed his own resignation on the top of the pile.

Many years later physicist Iggy Foster admitted to his colleagues that he was one of the two who did not write a letter of resignation. "The importance of this place as an institution of great promise was not worth the chance of interrupting it," he recalled, "even for that principle. What I wanted to do was wait, and we did wait."[83]

But most of the professors clearly felt that the principle and the reality of racism were worth the fight. "Nothing solidified that faculty, and I think the school, more than that experience," says Bevan. "I mean, it *solidified*." This FPC faculty, who could argue over whether to read *Hamlet* before *Oedipus*, who could disagree wildly over whether a student should be expelled for maiming a cat, who could fight so loudly about the curriculum that students overhearing the conversation were afraid—this faculty, all white and many southern though they were, found one voice on the issue of integration. And that voice said, "The time is now."

It was a strong statement to make in 1962 in St. Petersburg. While the struggle for rights for black citizens already had a long history, the South was still deeply segregated, even eight years after the Supreme Court's ruling against separate but equal public schools and six years after the bus boycott in Montgomery. St. Pete had a history of cross burnings on black-owned property and squalid living conditions for African-Americans, and in 1962 it still had segregated schools and neighborhoods. The full force of the civil rights movement, with its sit-ins, nonviolent demonstrations, voter registration drives, Freedom Riders, tear gas, high-powered water hoses, church bombings, and police dogs, was just beginning to mount.

While there's no disputing that Florida Presbyterian College was started by whites primarily with white students in mind, the faculty were bound to change that. Like the abolitionists before them, they saw it as their Christian duty, as the morally right thing to do. They believed the church-related college could not be what it claimed to be if it did not accept all qualified applicants. "It was as if the board of trustees didn't have the same vision that the faculty had and the same understanding of the faith," says Katharine Meacham.

As academics, they believed in the importance of providing a high-quality education to any students who were capable of doing the work, no matter whether they were Cuban refugees, Hungarian freedom fighters, or blacks from the nearby neighborhood. As founders of an institution intended to inspire change in higher education nationwide, they could not stand by and watch their college fall victim to old patterns and closed-minded attitudes. Although they did not yet have the rhetoric to discuss the value of diversity in the classroom, they knew a liberal arts education meant considering all points of view.

Other southern white colleges were integrating by the early 1960s. Wake Forest began accepting black students in 1960. In 1961 Tulane University in New Orleans sought a court ruling to permit the admission of black students, since its founding donors had stipulated that their grants were for the education of "young white persons." Emory University in Atlanta (in 1962) and Rice University in Houston (in 1963) also went to court specifically to get permission to admit black students.[84] The University of Mississippi admitted its first black student in 1962. When the University of Georgia admitted two African-American students in 1961, the FPC faculty wrote a joint letter to that university to express their support and appreciation for the decision.

Many of the faculty and students at Florida Presbyterian developed their beliefs about integration from their personal experiences. Ken Keeton had grown up in the segregated South, and it had made him an activist for civil rights. He tells a story of driving a moving van one summer after college with a black coworker. "He was never allowed to stay with me, nor could he eat with me, and I would have to go in and get his food and bring it out to the truck. One time we were driving to a mountain town in Kentucky, and we arrived late and were very tired, and I tried to get him a room with me, and they said, 'No black person has ever stayed overnight in this town.'

"And I said, 'Well, this is going to be an exception, because we're tired and I have no other place to go. We have to stay here. We have to unload this truck tomorrow, and he has no place to go.'

"So finally the guy put him in a broom closet upstairs and said, 'Okay, but you have to get him out before daylight.' I think that was the crowning incident in my realization as a southerner that the blacks were mistreated in the country."

FPC's first students were also well aware of the issue. Grover Wrenn says the teaching at FPC did not wrench him out of a familiar way of looking at the world, but it helped make sense of confusions he'd had about his upbringing in the South.

It made me in some ways more comfortable. I grew up thirty-two miles from Greensboro, North Carolina, where the first sit-in demonstrations at the Woolworth's lunch counter began in 1960. I grew up in the segregated south.

My parents, who were loving parents and devoted Christians, had taught me what they knew and believed, but that included things that I was just perplexed by. As a young person in the church, I had an opportunity to work with and know a number of young ministers in North Carolina with whom I had discussions about the race issue. I was very troubled by it. . . .

My mother was educated as a health care professional and, to her dying day, if she had help in the yard and maybe the house, sometimes from a white man and sometimes from a black man, she was always courteous to hired help, but when she fed the African-Americans, she would always boil the dishes. It was something that she had learned, and it was a prejudice that she had maintained.

My father built his doctor's office in the early 1950s, when he returned from his post-graduate work in ophthalmology, and it was just a couple of blocks from where I went to school. There were two waiting rooms—one said "colored," one said "white." They had separate entrances from the outside. What confused me was there was only one doctor, and he treated all the patients the same, but there was this separation out front.

I went to all-white public schools. We had the separate but equal doctrine. There were two school buildings built in Siler City at the same time. One was a first- to twelfth-grade school for black kids. The other was a white high school. . . . The two school buildings had been built with the same blueprints at the same time. One had been cared for because white kids went to it. The other had not been because black kids went to it. [After integration], when it was time for white kids to go to the school that black kids had attended, it was deemed not good enough. It was bulldozed, and a new school was built. That was separate but equal?

Those were very confusing lessons. I had a hard time sorting that out. But when I came to FPC, I saw faculty living out their views and commitments in a way that didn't have those inconsistencies.

When he was a student at FPC, Wrenn stood in long lines at the theaters in St. Petersburg to protest segregation at the movies. "I'd get up to the window and say, 'I'd like to buy two tickets.' And the white girl on the other side of the window would say, 'And who are the tickets for, sir?' And I'd say, 'My friend and me.' And there was a black person behind me, and they wouldn't sell me the tickets. So we'd go to the back of the line, and stand in line again."

When Wrenn, who was in North Carolina between his sophomore and junior years, heard about the decision of FPC's board from a fellow student, he remembers helping lead "a drive among students to resign. I wrote a letter to Bevan, and I wrote other students, saying that I was resigning as a student from the college. I did not yet know that the faculty was resigning as well."

"If the board would have stood their ground after getting all the resignations," says Bevan, "I do not believe FPC would be here today."[85]

Kadel remembers that none of the letters of resignation were to go into effect immediately. "But as soon as they could find opportunity to relocate, it was their intention to leave the college." Kadel reported this to the acting board chairman, Colin English, and suggested that English appoint four board members to a special committee, to which Kadel would appoint four faculty members (Bob Meacham, Ashby Johnson, Iggy Foster, and John Dixon). "This group of people, meeting with me, would wrestle over the next six months until the fall meeting of the board to find a resolution to the problem."

The first meeting of the ad hoc committee did not bode well. Kadel remembers, "I asked all present if they would be willing to work together to solve the problem. The board members indicated they would. The faculty members said they would not. They said that a young man had been hurt and that this was not a Christian thing and that they would not be satisfied unless this young man were admitted to the college. At this time, Colin English rose and left the room, saying to me before he left, 'You have my authority to accept all of the resignations that you have and I'll help you build another faculty of greater quality.'

"When he left the room I said to those remaining, 'If we are going to say to ourselves and to the community and to the world that the Christian college has no answer to this kind of conflict, then I think that it would be just as well if we left at this point.' And then one of the faculty said very strongly, 'Mr. President, if you are willing to assume full responsibility for the damage which has been done to this young man and full responsibility for its impact on the life of the college . . . then and only then am I willing to stay and work with you.' So said the other faculty."

The committee continued to meet throughout the summer. In September 1962, at a faculty meeting, they presented a draft resolution that would no longer allow FPC to deny admission based on race. The resolution would be presented to the board at its October meeting, where Kadel told the faculty he expected "favorable Board action" and "would not settle for anything less." The faculty broke into applause.

"People I talked with never really assumed we were going to lose," says Bouwman.

Even Ashby Johnson slowly came around: "By the time he left this institution," Johnson would later say of President Kadel, "I thought he had developed into one of the very best college presidents an institution could have."[86]

While Philip Lee, who had resigned as board chairman in May but remained active on the board, was not involved with the ad hoc committee, he admitted fifteen years later that Kadel "really had to educate us [the board] on this matter before he was able to progress much. . . . He played it, in my opinion, somewhat, you could say . . . coy in his timing of this thing. He timed it in a way that was not offensive, and he was able to bring pressure where he realized that there was an opportunity for pressure to be brought. And very slowly he changed and turned this thing all the way around. And he retained to my best recollection the loyalty of each member of the board. . . . I know he changed me around so that I thought so much of him that I bowed to his greater and wider scope of knowledge."

Another trustee (and future chairman of the board), Robert Sheen, supported integration from the start. His own company, Milton Roy, had declared since 1954 that it would not tolerate racial discrimination. But he remembers that some board members saw the college "as a possible vehicle and as a frontier to hold the line." Says Sheen, "It had to be a question of evolution on the board, and some of those trustees who felt that would be the case quickly saw they had a losing battle and either joined with us or dropped out."[87]

In October 1962 the board voted unanimously that application for admission to Florida Presbyterian College would be considered "without regard to race, color, or creed."

The decision came too late for Howard Kennedy, the young man who had hoped to attend FPC. He had already joined the army. But his application was an early brick in the pathway to civil rights. And those who fought for him would never be the same.

Shortly after this incident, the *St. Petersburg Times* reporter Lowell Brandle suddenly died of a heart attack, leaving behind a wife and eleven-year-old daughter. Kadel and the board voted to honor Brandle's memory with a full scholarship for his daughter when she reached college age, if she qualified for admission.

Three years later, in March 1965, German professor Ken Keeton, philosophy professor Keith Irwin, and chaplain Alan Carlsten drove all night to participate in the civil rights march organized by Martin Luther King Jr. in Selma, Alabama. Keeton remembers they "got together within a couple of hours after King's plea for marchers. We left at night, drove through to Selma in time for the march. We were again stopped at the bridge but with no violence to the marchers. A minister was shot, however, after the march was ended."[88]

Upon their return home the *St. Petersburg Times* wrote about their experience. They were invited to speak at black churches. Keeton felt the march was a "culmination" of all his efforts at integration and was "just something I had to do."

But not everyone respected their participation. The faculty received hate mail that, Keeton says, "terrified my wife and children." Donors to the college pressured Kadel to fire the men. Some pledges made to the college were withdrawn. Appalled by such reactions, a former newspaper publisher, Thomas Dreier, announced a $100,000 gift to FPC in answer "to those who have criticized the college because its faculty members had the courage to express their feelings at Selma." Said Dreier, "Gifts to colleges should be just as free as the minds of professors of the colleges should be free."[89]

Many years later founding faculty member John Satterfield wrote a speech for the governor of North Carolina, Robert Scott, in which he said, "Americans do not bring forth children as a gift to the nation, they bring forth a nation as a gift to their children." The line is attributed to Scott in his biography, but Satterfield knows it's his own writing. "Did it have any effect anyway?" he asks. "Of course not, but it had some effect on me. I thought I'd said something that was right."

CHAPTER 10

Building a Campus

It's amazing—to paraphrase Churchill—how so few did so much with so little money.

Bill Wilbur

The sun shone bright and hot, the air smelled of salt and sweat, and the sand shifted under high-heeled shoes as two thousand people gathered on September 24, 1961, at the new campus of Florida Presbyterian College for a ceremonial groundbreaking. Almost two hundred shovels, decorated by colleges and universities throughout the nation and sent as gifts to the new college, were handed out to students, faculty, and administrators. Lined up in orderly rows, they dug into the sandy soil that would soon be the site of Dendy-McNair Auditorium. FPC's choir, in matching red robes and white stoles, sang for the event. Various dignitaries said a few words from a covered platform.

When President Kadel stood to address the crowd, he began with a passage from Matthew 7:24–27—Jesus' closing words to the Sermon on the Mount: "Anyone who hears these words of mine and obeys them is like a wise man who built his house on rock. The rain poured down, the wind blew hard against that house. But it did not fall, because it was built on rock. But anyone who hears these words of mine and does not obey them is like a foolish man who built his house on sand. The rain poured down, the rivers flooded over, the wind blew hard against that house, and it fell."

"We couldn't get over it," laughs Bill Wilbur. "Here we were, digging in the sand, and he's talking about the foolish man who builds his house on sand."

The rest of Kadel's speech that day has not survived. He surely chose the text to get people's attention and to bring laughter to the occasion. But he must have also interpreted it so as to inspire confidence at the wisdom of the founding of this college. Perhaps he focused on the elements that would make up the solid foundation of a campus built on sand: its people, community support, faith in God, commitment to vision.

Over the next seven years as president, Kadel might sometimes have wondered if he was a foolish man to undertake this challenge, but the groundbreaking was the start of so many building projects that he would have little time for doubt for many months to come. In addition to the auditorium, simultaneous construction began on the library, a two-story classroom building, residential units, and the dining hall.

Faculty were involved in the design of the library and of their particular teaching facilities. While architectural notes emphasize the value of open designs that make the most of the climate and the waterfront, the final buildings, with flat roofs, brick exteriors, few views of the water, and enclosed spaces to keep in the air conditioning seem to have lost much of that original vision. Early architectural ideas for the chapel, however, quote Kadel as saying "there is a value in seeing each other," and this appears to have stuck: the chapel, built in 1967, has a circular design that encourages worshippers to look at one another.

As deans of students, Tom West and Frances Whitaker contributed ideas for the dormitories, and they supported the concept of a cluster of small "houses" around a central lounge area. Each house would be given its own name (for example, Gandhi House, Ibsen House, and Dante House) so that students would develop a shared identity within their house— something that would enhance competition in intramural sports, point the way to parties, and encourage supportive relationships among students.

The college community began using the new campus in the fall of 1962, but not all the buildings were complete, so much of that year was characterized by bus rides between the two campuses. All students began to attend classes on the new campus that fall, but only some of the young men actually moved into the dorms.

Dick Huss, a founding freshman, remembers that transitional time: "We got back here in the fall of '62, and there was nothing prepared. The dormitories were not complete; the cafeteria was not complete. We had no electricity after ten o'clock when the generators shut down. We had no furniture— you had your mattress on the floor, and you lived out of a suitcase. We had very few desks. There were only men out here on the campus. [The staff] would truck the food from the Bayboro campus to this campus, and we would then go to breakfast in our skivvies and pajamas and sit and eat scrambled eggs and wet toast off paper plates, seated around the cafeteria construction site on bricks and stuff. 'Every day was a picnic at FPC' was our slogan." He remembers a lot of rain and no walkways, so the grounds became like a swamp. But he also remembers it was still a wild place, with foxes and raccoons going by. "We didn't realize how good it was."[90]

By the beginning of the fourth academic year (fall 1963) all the students were moved in, the cafeteria was serving meals, the faculty all had offices and classrooms on campus, and the era of the interim campus had come to an end. On November 22 of that year Dendy-McNair Auditorium was filled to capacity for the first time when a memorial service was held for President John F. Kennedy.

That same fall FPC got a new athletic director, James Harley. Billy Wireman, though not yet thirty years old, had moved from athletics into a more administrative role and was helping Kadel with development efforts.

Wireman remembered Harley from when they were both graduate students at Peabody College. He knew Harley was a strong leader, excellent coach, and solid Christian. He also knew it would take some work to entice Harley away from his current position as director of athletics at Miami Dade Community College, which had also just opened its doors in 1960 but which had a much bigger budget, brand-new facilities built with state money, scholarships to lure top athletes, and a student population that was doubling every semester. By its third semester Miami Dade had six thousand students, and Harley (all of twenty-eight years old) had to hire fourteen additional staff members immediately. He even tried to hire Billy Wireman, who turned him down.

Harley was born in 1933 into a Presbyterian family of six kids and a long history as white southerners. He grew up on a dairy farm in Sparta, Georgia, where he hunted, fished, and played baseball with boys from the black families who helped on his parents' farm. He was playing football by the age of twelve, but when his growth spurt hit, he reached six foot one and found his "beating pulse" in basketball. Harley was president of his sixty-student high school class every year. After serving two years in the military, he finished college at Georgia Southern, where he met his wife, Mary Alice. He coached basketball and baseball at a junior college in Georgia before moving to Miami, where he was quickly exposed to a community rich with diversity—and highly segregated.

When Wireman called about the job at FPC, Harley was inexplicably tempted. "I always wanted to work in a small college," he remembers. "I never thought I would be where we didn't have anything, I mean no facility, no gym, no scholarships, no nothing."

His colleagues at other Florida colleges cautioned him against the move. Why would he want to leave a promising career at Miami for a school whose future athletic fields were currently a sandy lot that flooded in heavy rains? He had seen the FPC basketball team play in a tournament, and he watched the baseball team during his visit to the FPC campus. "It was a standard that I wasn't accustomed to," he remembers.

"But I kept saying, 'But it fits my career goals.'" When he told his mother—an active Presbyterian—about his interview at FPC, she said, "That's Bill Kadel's college," and encouraged him to take the job.

Harley remembers his interview with Kadel with a chuckle.

When I came over here to look at the job and the place, the big thing was, "You're going to have to pass the Kadel test." I kept hearing that from everybody—Have you had the Kadel test yet? So I was waiting for my appointment with Dr. Kadel. Dr. Bevan had prepped me a little bit, and Dr. Wireman had prepped me a little bit, but I wasn't quite ready for what happened. Stepping out of Dr. Kadel's office was John Ferguson, who became a professor of biology, a really good professor, a Cornell grad. Dr. Kadel brings the folder of John Ferguson to Dr. Bevan and says how wonderful this Cornell man would be for our faculty, giving the thumbs up.

Now, I had my session with Dr. Kadel, and he opens very, very nice. Then he says, "Do you believe in Jesus Christ? Why do you believe in Jesus Christ?" And he just went on. He was three questions ahead of me before I could get my answers out. And I'm thinking, "I don't know how I'm doing, but I don't think I'm doing very well." I did the best I could without choking up. And when he finishes the interview with me, he takes my folder to Dr. Bevan and says, "He'll do."

Harley ended up directing the athletic program at FPC for the next thirty-nine years, coaching over four hundred winning basketball games and becoming a highly respected figure in college athletics at the state and national level.

After he bought a house in St. Pete in the spring of 1963, he stopped by Bevan's office to report his new address. "I'm awfully glad you found a place," said Bevan, "but I should tell you that if we don't get sixty new students between now and July 1, we don't open in the fall." Harley and Wireman immediately hit the road together and personally recruited twenty-eight of the required sixty. Harley was relieved to still have a job come September.

FPC's focus on learning was part of the attraction for Harley. He quickly started a regular habit of attending lectures, plays, and performances on campus. He read an occasional book from the Western Civ syllabus. He taught a one-month class on anatomy and kinesiology. When he took the basketball team out of state to larger cities, he organized team trips to museums or historical sites. And he always let his athletes put course responsibilities ahead of practice.

In his first year Harley coached Rich Miller, a founding freshman who became FPC's star basketball player those first four years. When he was a senior, his team was still hosting other teams at a local junior high school gym. During a game against Florida Southern, Miller was at the free throw line when Harley overheard an opponent razzing Miller for playing for such a small, unknown school.

"What are you doing here?" said the player.

"I'm getting an education," said Miller. "What are you doing over at Florida Southern?"

The exchange reinforced why Harley had decided to come to FPC. "Selling the academic program was easy," he remembers. "Selling the athletic program was tougher." With no athletic scholarships to offer and limited facilities, Harley was turned down by a lot of student-athletes he wanted. But those who came were the kind of thinking, caring, hardworking students he ultimately wanted on his teams.

That included Harry Singletary, the first black student to graduate from FPC (in 1968). He was a fine basketball player who strengthened Harley's resolve to fight for racial integration. They both received hate mail from Ku Klux Klan members for having a black player on the FPC team. "Harry handled it so much better than I did," says Harley. "His answer was, 'They're ignorant.'"

Harley remembers a late team dinner at a diner off Interstate-75 after FPC had won an away game against a Tennessee college. "In walks the biggest, meanest looking sheriff you have ever seen in your life. I mean, if you've ever wanted to paint a picture of the southern, 'you're-in-a-heap-of-trouble-boy' type guy, that was him. He put his hands on his hips, and he just looks at Harry Singletary. Harry said, 'Coach, I think we better get out of here.' So we got up and left."

Singletary went on to become secretary of the Florida Department of Corrections. Harley is proud of the contribution he and his athletes made to integrating college sports in Florida and elsewhere. "We integrated the gymnasium at Washington and Lee in the heart of the confederacy," he remembers of one trip to Lexington, Virginia. "They had never had black students come and play. People were hanging off the windows outside to see that game."

Harley would have to wait until 1969 before FPC had its own gymnasium on campus. But by the mid-1960s the campus had four complete academic buildings with laboratories and classrooms, administration buildings, the chapel, a student union, a music center with soundproof studios, and several complexes of student residences with four two-story "houses" in each complex.

It would take a little longer to build the theatre and art buildings, but as art professor Jim Crane remembers, "Everything was growing together, and you didn't feel deprived as much as you felt anticipatory: 'When we do this and when we get this space...' That was a very valuable thing, and students responded to it."

A complete and more conventional campus obviously changed the community life of the college. In many ways it was, of course, much improved. Everyone had more space to do things, inside and out. It became easier to court donors and recruit students when they could be hosted at a college with its own permanent location of brand-new buildings. Faculty, administration, and staff could settle in more to their offices and plan farther into the future.

At the same time, as people became more self-sufficient, they became less group oriented. Harley began to miss talking about an upcoming game with his colleagues or listening to Fred White's witticisms at common coffee breaks. "When nobody had coffee in the office, you had to go over to the snack bar," he says. "There were those kinds of conversations that we don't get anymore. Now everybody's driving to the mailbox, and they have delivery service, and you have your own coffee pots. When we didn't have a drama building, we didn't have a music building, we didn't have an athletic building, we had to help each other."

The adaptability required on a fledgling campus is most dramatically portrayed in Jim Crane's memories of the art program at FPC. Crane was hired in 1963, when John Dixon (the art historian portrayed as Whistler's mother in one of Satterfield's lectures) left the college. Crane was not an art historian but a practicing artist, originally from Michigan, who was chairman of the art department at Wisconsin State College. Dean Bevan found him through *Motive* magazine—a high-quality, thought-provoking, and arts-promoting publication of the Methodist Student Movement of the Board of Education of the Methodist Church. Crane had published cartoon drawings with witty social commentary in *Motive* for several years.

Bevan wanted a working artist on the faculty. Crane remembers, "Bevan said, 'This is such a heavily verbal place. We've got to have more that students can do with their hands, that's concrete.'" Another *Motive* artist, Bob Hodgell, who produced droll prints and paintings, often with religious themes, also taught in the art program as a kind of artist-in-residence. Another artist and the managing editor at *Motive*, Peg Rigg, eventually joined them, too.

Crane, at thirty-six years of age, was the only one of the three with college teaching experience. But none of them could possibly have been prepared for an art program with no studio, no classrooms, and no equipment. Their first gathering place was a section of the newly built library, walled off with a temporary partition, which allowed "not an awful lot more than drawing," Crane remembers. But they did hang art exhibits on the library walls.

They also hosted exhibits from local artists. Crane remembers one show in particular, by a Tampa artist, which included a piece titled "Interesting Object": "The artist had a bag of plaster of Paris and he had a big tube, and he stuck the tube into the plaster of Paris, so it looked like male genitalia. One afternoon, Bill Kadel brought through a group of church people, and I think he nearly had a fit, because he had no idea there was anything like that there."

Bevan later asked Crane, "If you have anything like that again, will you please give us advance warning so we don't take tours to it?"

Shortly after that, the art program moved into a floor of James House—one of the dorm houses that was not yet needed as a residence. The art faculty and their students were offered a space that included dorm rooms, hallways, and a central lounge. Crane remembers touring it with Hodgell and Bevan. "We said, 'We'll take it!' Then Bevan left, and I said to Bob, 'How are we going to teach classes in a dorm room?' And he said, 'We won't teach classes. We'll just give everybody a studio and tell them to go to work.'" Crane has never heard of another college that provides private studios to undergraduate art students.

About half the students dropped out of the art program, not knowing what to do with the space, the freedom, and the responsibility. "But the ones who stayed," says Crane, "thought, 'Wow, my own studio!' Well, of course, they turned them into their pads." Students worked all hours on their art and met regularly in the lounge for critiques. Unlike in other art programs, where the critiques would focus on one medium—a painting critique, for example—these discussions reviewed whatever the students were producing, from photographs and clay to watercolors and drawing.

Of course, students did not always take the approach seriously. "They would bring in works that they had spent ten or fifteen minutes on, and they would talk and talk and talk," Crane remembers. "Bob taught an Introduction to Art course, and people would be asked things like, 'Bring in a work of art and explain why you picked this out.'. . . Somebody brought in himself and said, 'I'm a work of art,' and then he defended that. Both of us were a little bit boggled by the audacity of these kids."

On the whole, however, Crane believes that the unusual circumstances fostered unusually positive results: "Students had to learn to articulate, better than most art students do, what they're about and to communicate that to another student who might not have any idea of the medium they're working in or what aesthetic problem they are solving or what they're trying to express." Art students developed an independence and ability to "work in a sustained way with a problem." Art majors were required to exhibit a "thesis show" in their senior year.

The approach also allowed the relatively small program of three faculty to offer only one art major—in studio work—instead of trying to offer specializations in art history, art education, or particular media. It meant that when students went off to graduate school in art, they weren't as technically skilled in particular forms as some other students, but they found that they could learn the skills quickly and unlike many of their peers, says Crane, they could "step into a studio and start to work."

(Bill Wilbur says his history majors also reported that they "may not have gotten such a tremendous depth in a particular discipline and may have been a little bit behind some of these other students who were in that particular discipline, but in the long run the broad interdisciplinary education put them way ahead of others.")

Jim Crane spent the rest of his career at FPC / Eckerd College. He laments the time spent in committee meetings instead of on his own artwork, but he thrived as a teacher of Western Civilization and Its Christian Heritage. In the early 1970s, when the college finally came around to building dedicated space for the art program, Crane and his colleagues insisted on maintaining the concept of private studios for students.

When the original buildings of the campus were completed, FPC was the first all-electric college in the country—a decision seen as ahead of its time technologically and one that "just cemented further the relationship between the college and the Florida Power Corporation," says FPC trustee Philip Lee. As the years went by, however, and the cost of electricity kept rising, it would turn out to be a foolish decision.

Some supporters of the college eventually thought it was foolish to build so much so quickly. Says Lee, "We tried to have the college grow too rapidly and we found ourselves almost in bankruptcy because of too many buildings. We had gone out on the limb for so many buildings that did not of themselves produce any revenue for paying off the obligation of such indebtedness. I believe that is one thing that, maybe, Dr. Kadel may have had a hand in. He was very, very ambitious for the college to grow and grow rapidly and, of course, without that ambition why we wouldn't be where we are today, but at the same time it was not too realistic."[91]

Trustee Robert Sheen agrees: "Dr. Kadel was most influential in raising money for the campus buildings, although most of the cost was financed with mortgage and bank debt. While we had a number of campaigns to raise additional funds, it soon became apparent that we were overbuilt and undercapitalized."[92]

Billy Wireman, FPC's second president, puts it this way: "We wanted it all and we wanted it all by noon tomorrow and we were willing to risk on the assumption that at some point quality and excellence would indeed attract dollars. And I think to some degree that was true, but I think all of us would agree that the early years were defined, to a large extent, by the sense of economic need. And I must say that as I look back on that situation, knowing what I know now, having been a college president myself for twenty-three years, that what Bill Kadel and Jack Bevan did in those early years, just keeping enough oxygen, enough cash to launch the effort, was nothing short of a miracle."[93]

Indeed, Kadel believed God would work miracles to keep the college alive. "He was so strong in the idea that this was God's mission, to have this college here," West recalls.

"He had a lot of faith that this college would go on and survive," says Bill Wilbur, "even when it looked pretty grim that it was financially not going to make a go of it. But he said, 'God wants this thing to go.' He must have lost sleep about it, but he never seemed to lose faith that it was going to survive."

Satterfield remembers Kadel as "a man who had faith much beyond mine. He believed that God was starting that college. He fully believed that. I don't think he ever changed that as long as he lived. I think he felt that he personally had that kind of a relationship with God. And he was persistent and just a bulldog. He was going to hang on, and he was going to win down there in the face of no matter what. And, boy, I have seen him when his chin was on the floor. He didn't know what to do. But, by morning, his chin was off the floor, and he was fighting again."

While early financial commitment to the college was strong and enthusiastic, once the school was up and running, finding enough support to pay the ever-increasing bills was a constant struggle. Indeed, people still joke that every time the St. Petersburg Times has run an article about the college, it has identified the school as "financially troubled Florida Presbyterian College" or "financially troubled Eckerd College."

Faced with early and ongoing financial concerns, Kadel surely did turn to God for help. The image has become part of the college's lore. Says West, "Every now and then, we were thinking we weren't going to be able to make the payroll, and Bill Kadel would go into a closet and pray. Emma Conboy, his secretary, would say, 'He's in the closet again.' And, lo and behold, the next day, a gift would come in. It would make the payroll. We never missed a payroll. He'd go out and pray with people in the churches, too."

"The story I heard," laughs Jim Crane, "is that every time Bill Kadel prayed, one of our donors died, and we inherited enough money to pay our bills."

In 1976 Ashby Johnson brought up the story of FPC's early and ongoing financial challenges with Alvin Eurich, the Ford Foundation officer who provided the first grants to the fledgling college. Johnson wanted to know if Eurich thought the college could have done anything better in those early years to avoid being in a constant state of financial crisis. Eurich essentially dismissed his worries, suggesting that it is the nature of our society that everyone, families and institutions, are always in a financial crisis.[94]

Such a perspective would have been of little comfort to those who felt the impact of the college's money problems. In a brief diary of events from 1961 Ken Keeton records, "Jack Bevan reported on Feb. 4 that we have 450,000 dollars rather than nothing, as had been rumored for two weeks." On April 21 Keeton writes, "Kadel announced to an angry faculty there would be no raises next year." And on April 25: "5% salary cut announced."

When publishers refused to send any more periodicals for the library because the bills had not been paid, someone discovered that the business manager was hiding invoices in a drawer of his desk because there was not enough money to cover them.

A memo from President Kadel to "Members of the College Community," dated November 9, 1967, is almost pathetic if it was not so indicative of real crisis: "Heretofore the college has held an annual Christmas party for the members of the college community, but because of budget revisions and cut-backs in all areas of the program, we are forced to forgo this activity this year and trust you will all understand."

Financial shortfalls in the early years created an undercurrent of anxiety and concern for the future that no doubt greatly worried the president and trustees. But the college continued on with its academic mission unabated, as students learned, questioned, awoke to new understandings, and eventually found themselves ready to graduate.

CHAPTER 11

Epiphanies

The purpose of FPC was not to give students the answer, but to give them the question: "How do I live?"

John Satterfield

When Carolyn Hall was a senior at FPC in 1964, she was walking from the library to the cafeteria when she experienced a sudden, overwhelming "feeling of wholeness, of being centered, of having grown so much, of being alive." She remembers feeling that "God was so present in everything. I felt like I was a child of God."

For Carolyn her four years at Florida Presbyterian College planted the seed for her future development as a person and for the ongoing spiritual journey of her life. "I can't say that it set the pattern for all my future learning," she says now. "I have definitely learned more and in different ways at other times in my life. But it was the impetus to look for that kind of depth in all of my learnings and my dealings with other people."

When she arrived at Pasadena Community Church in her black gown and mortar board for graduation ceremonies, she was one of sixty-five founding freshmen who had made it through all four years. She was excited about her next step in life—

a Fulbright grant to teach English and study in France for a year. But she was also sad to leave behind the intense relationships and experiences of this institution she had helped to create.

When the faculty arrived for the first commencement of FPC, decked out in their academic regalia, Bevan told them, "Fall in line anywhere. No hierarchy."

One can only imagine the pride and wonder Bevan and Kadel felt that day, conferring degrees on their fiddler crabs, now college graduates. As the ages-old academic tradition unfolded before them, they could not have helped being moved by this ultimate result of their years of effort.

The administration and faculty had every reason to bust buttons over the students' accomplishments. Ten graduated with high honors. More than 60 percent went on to graduate and professional schools. Three won Fulbright fellowships, two won Woodrow Wilson fellowships, and three won NDEA (National Defense Education Act—for graduate study in science, engineering, and foreign languages) fellowships.[95] Hugh McEniry, dean of the College of Liberal Arts at Stetson University, chaired the Woodrow Wilson fellowship committee and reviewed the applications from FPC students. He called Bevan to say, "I don't know what it is you're doing, but what we saw—we couldn't believe it! Whatever you're doing, I want to learn about it."

One graduate was accepted to Duke Medical School when only eighty of nine hundred qualified applicants got in. Other graduate school destinations included Harvard University, the New School for Social Research, Northwestern, Union Theological Seminary, Emory, and the University of Virginia. A music major who went on to the University of Pittsburgh wrote John Satterfield that the faculty there said she was the best prepared first-year graduate student they had ever taught.

Several women graduates went on to teach school in Pinellas County or elsewhere. One graduate joined the Peace Corps.

The members of the founding class of Florida Presbyterian headed in all these impressive directions, despite the fact that FPC was not yet officially accredited by the Southern Association of Colleges and Secondary Schools. (FPC would receive full accreditation in 1966, in the shortest time possible under the association's rules.) Bevan spent quite a bit of time on the phone that fourth year telling FPC's story to graduate school deans and scholarship committees, to make sure his students would not be penalized.

Not all the first class were stellar graduates, but Bouwman thinks, "Because of the intensely personalized relationships between the faculty and that freshman class, even those who were not so able, who by objective standards would not have measured up, came right along with the others and did satisfactorily."

"It is my firm conviction," Ashby Johnson said later, "that the students who attended Florida Presbyterian College, starting in the fall of 1960, and for the next, oh, four to five years, received as good an educational challenge and experience as any comparable group of students in the United States."[96]

With the graduation of its first class, Florida Presbyterian College had completed a full cycle in the life of a college. The job now before its faculty and administration was to complete that cycle over and over for subsequent generations of students forever. Of course, it had to continue to grow—more buildings for the campus, more students to fill its halls and classrooms, more faculty to teach them.

By 1966 the college had 61 faculty, 810 students, and a $14 million campus. That year a brief article in *Time* magazine announced the college's accreditation and gave FPC's public relations staff one of its favorite quotes: "From vacant lot to excellence in just six years."[97]

As the college was growing, its academic program was diversifying. Jim Carlson came in the fall of 1964 to start FPC's theatre program. He left Hamline University in St. Paul, Minnesota, because the administration there was not too sure about Carlson's choice of repertoire, including the first American performance of one of Bertolt Brecht's works. A fellow Hamline professor, Peter Meinke (who would follow Jim to FPC), says the president at Hamline asked Carlson, "Why are you putting on all these Commie plays?"

Dean Bevan was looking for an intellectual theatre program that would emphasize cutting-edge works, not pop musicals, so Carlson's interests fit the bill. Bevan was also impressed that Carlson was co-editor of *Religious Theater* magazine.

With no theatre building until 1969, students performed plays in Dendy-McNair Auditorium. Carlson thought the "program of the theatre should be an extension of liberal education," and he often chose works that complemented learning in the Core courses. While the auditorium had its structural drawbacks for live performance, Carlson liked that "you saw a play by Bernard Shaw in the same place you were during your Core lectures." He found that issues taken up in Western Civ would "echo and re-echo" in a play and create "a very intense experience" of the values students were exploring in a more theoretical way in other classes.

In the early years FPC did not offer a major in theatre, so students performed and produced plays as a sideline to their other studies. They flocked to Carlson as a professor, mentor, and friend, impressed by his intellect and inspired by his radical perspectives. It was in Carlson's house where Watson experienced those great meals with other faculty and students and that rare sense of being part of an intellectual community.

Many of Carlson's students remained close friends throughout his life. Carlson stayed with the theatre program until 1976, when he left the college in protest of a decision by the board—over faculty and student disapproval—to allow an ROTC program on campus. He eventually retired to St. Petersburg, where he continued to entertain and interact with former students and colleagues.

After giving his so-called Quaker blessing during his first visit to FPC, Peter Meinke arrived from Hamline in 1966, at the age of thirty-four, to start the college's creative writing program. He had recently completed a Ph.D. degree in English literature and was just beginning to read his own poetry publicly. He still considered himself a teacher who wrote poetry, rather than a poet who taught, and that's what Bevan wanted.

Meinke remembers meeting with Bevan to discuss plans for the writing program: "He paced around, and he was smoking—we all smoked in those days. I thought he was going to set the place on fire, he was so wild and walking around in circles. 'We're going to start the first undergraduate writing major. You're going to do this. And we're going to have a first-rate literary magazine, and you're going to help start this up. We're going to have poetry readings.' And I said, 'Yeah, okay, sure.' A lot of it came to pass, actually. I don't know if it was the first undergraduate creative writing major, but it certainly was one of the earliest."

Meinke developed a major that was essentially a study of English literature with a few writing courses in poetry, fiction writing, drama writing, and children's writing. He set aside a small room in one of the academic buildings as a "writing workshop" for students to read and comment on one another's poems and stories and for visiting poets and authors to read their work. He didn't intend that creative writing majors should have to become professional writers, just that "students would come out with a good grasp of English and American literature and an ability to express themselves."

Sterling Watson came to FPC as a student the same year Meinke arrived. He played on the baseball team and competed with vigor in intramural sports, got involved in the theatre program, and courted a girl he had known from high school. But in his studies he was "uncommitted, doing shabby work, and feeling bad about it." Literature came to the rescue: "I remember I had what I have called an epiphany. I was skipping class. I think it was a history class, and I was a history major, which I was doing just because my brother was one. I was lying in my bunk in the dorm, skipping class and reading a novel, and suddenly it hit me that that could be my life. The thing I was doing when I was hiding from what I should be doing could be the thing that I should be doing. So I changed my major and started being what we called an English major in those days." He took a winter term writing workshop in which he wrote some short stories that were "widely admired" among his peers.

Watson was one of the rare literature and writing students at the college who would go on to become a professional writer and distinguished novelist. Now a longtime professor of creative writing on the same campus where he had his epiphany, Watson says most of his students do not continue in writing careers, even though they are always glad they majored in writing. In a survey of the alumni of his and Meinke's program, conducted in the late 1990s, they found that students loved their education in creative writing. "They felt it had been tremendously valuable to them," says Watson, "because now they were attorneys, now they had their own businesses, now they were consultants. It was such a great preparation for so many things."

A 1964 "Special Graduation Issue" of FPC's newsletter to the larger community completes its story of the first graduating class by saying, "The true test will come over the next 15 or 20 years . . . as those young people take their place in society, and make the influence of their ideas and judgments felt."

After her year in France, Carolyn Hall (now Horton) became a teacher of French, Spanish, and Latin and served as dean of faculty at a private, college preparatory school in St. Petersburg. In the 1990s she received training in pastoral care for hospital patients and directed a volunteer pastoral care program until retiring to the North Carolina mountains.

Grover Wrenn, with his wife and two children to support, left FPC in 1963 and finished his last year of a chemistry degree at Clemson University in Georgia, where his family could live in affordable married-student housing. The difference between FPC's culture of learning and what he saw at Clemson—widespread cheating, no interest in learning for learning's sake—was a shock for him.

Although Wrenn "revered" the time he had spent at FPC, he lost contact with the college for the next thirty years. Meanwhile, he earned a master's degree in public health and environmental science at the University of North Carolina, worked for the Occupational Safety and Health Administration, and then co-founded a highly regarded international environmental consulting firm in Washington, DC, that eventually went public. He was brought back to the college in the 1990s as a trustee. He carries the hope that the college can "continue to attract and serve bright young people who are seeking a traditional residential college for undergraduate liberal arts learning, which I think is the most powerful foundation for living the life of the mind and the life of the spirit in a complex and changing world."

Watson jokes that the college attracts the brightest and most promising young people from every Panhandle town in Florida. "Half of them left town with the curses of their elders ringing in their ears: 'What are you doing, wasting your life on that little place down there?' But a little music up in the pine trees says, 'Come here, come here, and you'll land something, something will change your life.'"

CHAPTER 12

In the Name of Higher Education

Shun not the struggle: face it, 'tis God's gift.

Rev. Maltie D. Babcock (1858-1901)

On a balmy evening in the late 1960s a debate was cooking at a meeting of the Pinellas County School Board, the board that oversaw St. Petersburg's schools. Poet and FPC professor Peter Meinke was there, along with several of his faculty colleagues. Whatever they were supporting, it was in opposition to the views of the conservative board. In the midst of the conflict another person in the audience leaped up and told the board, "I want you to know that the whole town is behind you, except for those idiots at Florida Presbyterian."

And the faculty yelled, "Yeahhhh!"

The college had grown a long way from the ideals of local businessmen when they lured the new institution to St. Pete with a community dinner at the Suwannee Hotel. The lavish attention the early college received from the local newspaper—from giant reproductions of campus drawings to pictures of faculty wives in the society pages—was replaced by critical letters to the editor. Says sociology professor Clark Bouwman,

"It became identified as a liberal institution, and, at that point, we lost our standing in the community to some degree."

The FPC faculty did not come to St. Petersburg to teach quietly in an ivory sunroom while fellow citizens suffered injustices. Beginning with the civil rights movement and building momentum with controversial guest lecturers, support of local labor actions, and eventually war protests, the difference between the dominant perspectives of the St. Pete community and the beliefs and behaviors of the college community grew starker.

"All of this was in the newspaper," says Katharine Meacham, "so that it looked as if we were a bunch of radicals. To us, we were doing what seemed the Christian thing to do."

Bouwman says it grew out of their definition of liberal arts as both an academic approach and a way of thinking: "Open minded, seeking to learn, willing to accept new and different means of learning, changing objectives as time went on—all of that was a part of liberality, plus the responsibility to be involved in that process."

West agrees. "We really had our struggles, because we were free thinking, open, moving away from any kind of prejudice. And, of course, in the community, you're going to have your people who don't like that kind of movement at all."

As a student, Watson felt that the residents of St. Pete viewed the college as "this sort of mysterious place out here, on the end of the peninsula. I think there was always a sense that there was excellence here, but I think there was also a sense that the college was a kind of a crucible of radicalism."

Several faculty were active in a 1968 strike of St. Petersburg's underpaid and mostly black sanitation workers. Clark Bouwman and his wife, Pat, walked with the workers every day for weeks from 22nd Avenue South to city hall. Martin Luther King Jr. had been assassinated earlier that year while in Memphis to support a garbage workers strike in that city. One afternoon during the St. Petersburg strike, King's brother came to make a speech to the striking workers on the steps of city hall, but the city tried to move the group away from that location. When the workers and their supporters refused to change course, a contingent of police officers from numerous cities appeared with shields to block the crowd's way.

Bouwman remembers everyone "sat down in the street and did not move and said, 'We're going this way, and we don't want to attack you, so we'll sit here until you let us through.' Whereupon city hall and their paddy wagons began arresting people for obstructing traffic in the street."

At that point Bouwman, who was there that day with Howard Carter and Peter Meinke, saw two men from the city council standing across the street. The three professors decided to go talk with them. "So we went across and introduced ourselves," says Bouwman, "and they said to us, 'You guys are just looking for publicity. You just want to get your picture in the paper. If you really meant this, you'd be out there in the street with those others who are getting arrested.' So we looked at each other and said, 'Well, if that's what they think, okay, we'll prove our point.' So we all three went out and sat down and shortly were arrested and hauled off and spent the night in jail. . . . Soon after that, the city gave in and admitted the sanitation workers back into their jobs."

For all the conflict between town and gown, positive influences ran both ways. Community leaders continued to make financial contributions that built the campus, provided scholarships for students, and supported new programs, while activities at the college brought new intellectual and cultural resources to residents.

Art professor Jim Crane points to several examples of the impact the college had on the arts in St. Petersburg. He and artist Bob Hodgell helped start a local art center and designed a program to help artists pursue their bachelor's degrees. They also opened the city's first gallery for modern art and helped develop a crafts cooperative. Art and drama students who have graduated and stayed in the area have opened pottery studios and theatre companies.

In more recent years, alumni have continued to influence the Tampa Bay area with their work. One graduate started a horseback riding program for disabled children, and another founded an organization that provides art and work experiences for mentally and emotionally disadvantaged residents. Others have led economic development and leadership programs for the City of St. Petersburg. And alumnus John Debevoise became senior minister at Tampa's leading Presbyterian church, Palma Ceia (where Bill Kadel served as pastor in the 1940s).

These contributions weren't always so evident, however, to church and civic leaders. As the sixties progressed, Tom West noticed that President Kadel "did a lot of preaching with different groups in the community, dealing with understanding and compassion for people."

Bill Wilbur's perception was that it was "tough" for Kadel at times "to come to grips with faculty people who were pretty individualistic and a lot of times maybe considered to be radical from his viewpoint. But he grew an awful lot, and he certainly was supportive of the faculty in many ways. And it cost him, I'm sure, a lot of anguish and maybe hostility from his community-at-large occasionally."

Delicate maneuverings were required to keep the church interested and involved without compromising the academic mission. "During the early years of the college," Kadel remembers, "I spent my time in interpreting both to the internal community and to the external community what I believed was the nature of a Christian college. After a while I decided that was not an appropriate title. I spoke rather of what Christians ought to do in the name of higher education."[98]

Billy Wireman was with Kadel at meetings where they were trying to interpret the college for church people. "He would be the first to say he didn't fully understand what was taking place there in terms of Christian witness," says Wireman. "Nonetheless he believed in the people. . . . I think we said we wished to be 'Christian in ways relevant to our time.' The perception of church-related colleges was that they were supposed to be sort of havens and oases for protecting the faith and not challenging it, and we weren't like that. And to our everlasting credit the college did stay related to the church, did take seriously its church-relatedness, and at the same time attempted to be true to its academic mandate."[99] The church, however, may not have been fully convinced; gifts from the Presbyterian Church in 1967 were the lowest in the college's history.

Even so, many early professors still praise the church and the trustees for not usurping the authority of the administration and faculty, for believing in the value of academic freedom, and for letting the college unfold with the times.

By 1967 the times were changing on college campuses all over the country. Already known for its political activism, Florida Presbyterian College was not immune to the student rights movement, with its disdain for authority, nor to the impact of drug use, sexual freedom, and the Vietnam War. "Kennedy's children" with their proper attire and dorm curfews and wide-eyed optimism had graduated and been replaced by students who were questioning or rejecting all previous conventions.

Some students were beginning to dress like hippies, including going to graduation barefoot, and such outward symbols of rebellion did not sit well with the larger community. Conversely, a 1968 suspension of several students suspected of using illegal drugs did not sit well with much of the college community. Billy Wireman remembers the college as "the Berkeley of the East before that was a compliment. You can't believe the kind of student dress and the student attitude. It wasn't happening just on our campus, but our liberal, progressive, open attitude invited that free spirit of a student."

Most FPC students were still excellent thinkers. When Bill McKee joined the faculty in 1967 to teach history, he found FPC's students to be "intellectually better than the students I had at Princeton."

But as they walked across their beautiful and mostly finished campus, Jack Bevan and Bill Kadel could not deny that FPC was a different place now from the institution they had nurtured into existence. They were exhausted from nearly a decade of nonstop work. They had met the challenges of founding the college and were ready for something different. God called them in new directions.

Bevan was the first to leave—in July 1967. In a memo to the trustees Kadel said the decision was met with "sadness and regret," that the college "shall always be in his debt," and that "the loss of Jack from our leadership team will be great."[100]

Bevan became dean at University of the Pacific in Stockton, California, which was experimenting with theme-based colleges within the larger university. After a short time there, he returned to Davidson College as dean of faculty, and he later helped transition the College of Charleston (in South Carolina) from a private to a state university. "He loved revamping programs," says his wife, Louise. She remembers a friend once teased Jack by saying, "If you get to heaven, the first thing you'll want to do is change the place." Jack responded, "They haven't done anything new in 1900 years. Maybe it's time."

After all the colleges and universities he served, Bevan still said in 1989, "I've never been with a sharper and more critical group of individuals who felt complete freedom in expressing themselves as at Florida Presbyterian / Eckerd College. I never went anywhere that I didn't compare where I was with Eckerd College."[101]

Bevan retired from the College of Charleston in 1986 and moved with Louise to her family's home in Sumter County, South Carolina. He immediately became an active volunteer, raising funds for Alzheimer's research, Habitat for Humanity, and a new retirement home; becoming Rotarian of the Year; and teaching Sunday School at a nearby Methodist church. He still visited Eckerd College for special occasions and alumni events, even near his death, when he was attached to an oxygen bottle and was no longer a bear of a man. On that day he talked about how much he enjoyed his time at FPC and how proud he was of the institution in the years since. Then his eyes filled with tears. "I'll see you on the other side," he said. Bevan died February 4, 2000.

Following on the heels of his longtime friend's resignation, John Satterfield made his own decision to leave FPC. Anxious to prove himself in college administration, he took a position as dean of faculty at Elmyra College and would eventually retire from higher education as president of Wagner College in Staten Island, New York. A 2003 interview with him provided some of the best material for this book. Satterfield died on September 17, 2004.

Bill Kadel left FPC in 1968. He confided to his family that he was getting hives from the stress of his work. "He told me he was just worn-out, just tired," says Wireman.

Sarah Dean came for a job interview as the new dean of women during Kadel's last days on campus. Robert Kennedy was assassinated the same weekend as her visit, so everyone was huddled around the television and "all to pieces about it." Dean remembers her brief meeting with Kadel: "I walked into his office, and he said, 'Young lady, are you a Christian?'

"I was caught off guard. I said, 'Yes, sir, I am.'

"He said, 'All right, that will just be fine.'

"That's the last I saw of him."

On May 31, 1968, Kadel sent a handwritten, mimeographed note to the members of the college community to say good-bye, thanking everyone for sharing "evidences of their affection" in "these days of emotion and change." In explaining his reluctant acceptance of the position of executive secretary of the Board of Christian Education for the Presbyterian Church (U.S.) in Richmond, Virginia, Kadel told the college, "The world must again be able to say, 'Behold how these Christians love one another.' Perhaps I can help."[102]

The new job was no less stressful for Kadel, because the board was being dismantled, and he had to reduce the staff there from 186 to 75 people. While in Richmond, the Kadels' youngest daughter, Mary, who had grown up on the Florida Presbyterian campus, finished high school and returned to St. Pete to attend FPC. When the troubling job for the Presbyterian Church was completed in 1971, the Kadels moved back to their home state of Pennsylvania, where Bill became president of Pittsburgh Theological Seminary until his retirement in 1978.

He retired to Florida—to Lake City in the north—and returned to the pulpit as an interim minister for small churches. His wife, Kay, remembers that the Presbytery had to rule that, since Bill was retired, he could not serve the same church more than six months. "They were supposed to try to get a permanent minister. But as long as he was the minister there, they didn't want to do anything about getting someone else."[103] He kept ministering until the pain of cancer was too great to ignore. Bill Kadel died in October 1990 at the age of seventy-six.

For several years in the 1980s, Kadel served as a member of the Eckerd College Board of Trustees. I was a student at Eckerd at that time. I remember his coming in to visit me at my work-study job at the William Luther Cobb Library when he was on campus for trustee meetings. To me it was just a friendly visit with my grandpa. To him it must have been further evidence of God's handiwork—this library, this campus, this college, he had built just kept going, and was now educating his granddaughter twenty years after his departure.

CHAPTER 13

Crisis and Change

There was a special aura, special mystique, around some of those early years. We knew at the time that we'd never recapture it. We could not perpetuate it indefinitely.

Ashby Johnson

"It was one of the shortest presidential searches in history," says Billy Wireman of his election as president of Florida Presbyterian College in 1968. Kadel announced his resignation on April 30, and Wireman was elected on May 3. "We didn't have time to find anybody else," Wireman remembers. "The college simply could not endure a twelve- to eighteen-month search" plus the transition time an outsider would have needed to establish himself as head of the college. FPC was too young and too financially unstable for a lengthy interruption of solid leadership. According to Wireman's recollections, the college had a $600,000 deficit and was one hundred students short of its necessary enrollment for the following fall.

Since his initial position directing physical education and coaching basketball at FPC, Wireman had moved up the ranks of college administration, serving as dean of men, director of teacher education, and eventually vice president for development. He had already been offered the presidency of a small Tennessee college when board president Philip Lee suggested FPC had bigger plans for him. When Lee announced the board's decision to a group of six hundred students and faculty in FPC's Fox Hall, the applause shook the windows.[104]

Wireman was only thirty-five years old, one of the youngest college presidents in the country. With his boyish face and modest height, he did not look the part of a college president, but the newspapers called him a natural born salesman with tireless energy. His early speeches and published writings reveal an intellectual, a thoughtful educator, and a visionary leader concerned with the public good. He compared FPC to the space flights that were taking off from Florida in those days—first was the launch, requiring "sheer, raw power," and now came the orbital mission calling for "a different kind of engineering."[105]

"Kadel and Bevan took it from zero to one," says Wireman, "and that was Herculean in its dimensions. I don't know how in the world they did it. But then, when I came along, it was a challenge to take it through that initial excitement, that promise, and hang on." He also recognized that students' expectations for their college experience were changing and that FPC's administration would have to be more accessible and more inclusive of students' perspectives in the future.

Wireman's dean of students, Sarah Dean, saw the same trends: "First was that very beginning period which must have been glorious, when everybody came together from all these wonderful places and created this. And then it got established and they got a campus, and then there's this change in society, this big era where the nation was just really teetering. . . . So it was a challenge to keep our faith and our commitment, all the time trying to raise money, but it was a time of enormous excitement."

As a product of FPC's earliest days, Wireman brought an attitude of innovation and understanding that helped the college through this challenging time. Says Wireman, "I have always seen education as a vehicle through which we're going to inculcate these very idealistic principles of freedom, justice, enlightenment, in the minds of young people. How else are you going to do it? It ain't gonna happen automatically, so you've got to be proactive, aggressive in having that as the basis for the education establishment in this country. And that's what I've tried to do, to provide an atmosphere of openness, freedom, where they're free to agree or disagree and choose, but then take a stand without being offensive and intrusive about it."

FPC students in the late 1960s and early 1970s gravitated toward openness and freedom and certainly were not afraid of taking a stand. But they didn't always avoid being offensive and intrusive either.

The Vietnam War weighed heavily on everyone's mind. Students organized a single-file march from campus to the downtown post office to mail letters of protest. "St. Petersburg citizens would swear at them, spit on them, yell obscenities at them," remembers Dean. Ken Keeton wrote letters on behalf of students to keep them from having to serve in the war. Bill Wilbur remembers seniors coming to him to discuss whether they should go to graduate school or try to go to Canada to avoid being drafted. Students burned their draft cards on campus.

After the shootings of students at Kent State, a group of FPC students, working through the night, covered the quadrangle of grass outside Brown Hall with small white crosses. "It was like a cemetery," Dean remembers. "All day, as people would come around the corners and walk into that area, there would just be a hush. There was a sense of deep agony over what was going on at that time."

Civil rights took on a more radical edge during these years. Dean remembers the pain she felt when a black student suggested she was racist, and Wireman remembers a young black woman saying to him, "You run this plantation." Says Wireman, "I still have some pretty deep scars from some things that kids did then."

In November 1971 two dozen African-American students locked themselves inside Brown Hall (where the student game room was located) for twenty-five hours. The sit-in began as a response to a conflict between a white employee in the game room and a small group of black students; it led to a charge of "institutional racism." The students eventually came out on their own with the assurance that they would participate on a committee with the administration to address issues such as recruiting more African-American students, professors, and staff; providing better financial aid to black students; and improving relations within the college community.[106]

As student rights rose on the political agenda, Dean worked with students to develop a "joint statement on student rights" and tried to provide them more decision-making power on campus.

When they were not protesting or causing consternation to the administration, students were still college kids, taking classes, studying into the wee hours, and hanging out. They watched old Bogart movies in Dendy-McNair Auditorium at night and went to the beach behind the abandoned Veterans Administration Building on St. Pete Beach (now revived as the Don CeSar Resort Hotel).

Few students had cars, remembers Sterling Watson, who says, "We were not anything like as inclined as students are now to get in a car and go somewhere. . . . We didn't go out clubbing. We didn't go to restaurants. . . . Most people I knew didn't have any money. . . . The campus was really a kind of isolated place. What we did at night was get together and talk. This has been a staple remark about college life for one hundred years—you learn more outside the classroom than you learn in. Well, you learn a lot if you're around a bunch of intelligent people and you're having conversations about interesting things."

Professors continued to seek close relationships with students in order to help them through troubling times and challenge them to learn. The faculty developed an official "mentoring" program that ensured each student was paired with a professor, who would not only advise about academic decisions but also listen to personal concerns and foster success throughout the student's college odyssey.

Tom West went to northern California in the late 1960s and "came back a different person." Not only was he fascinated with the counterculture, but his approach to psychology was influenced by Carl Rogers and Abraham Maslow to the extent that he realized "psychology is not to diagnose and to manipulate and control people, but is to help people discover what they could potentially be, respecting people and their abilities to learn and develop themselves." A few years later West returned to the Bay Area with a group of students, where they had the chance to meet Rogers and Maslow.

While some faculty became more experimental in the later 1960s and 1970s, FPC's curriculum wavered between innovative, nontraditional approaches and a tendency toward the status quo in higher education. New faculty were hired right out of graduate school who had little background in nontraditional forms of learning. While the core curriculum and January term remained, disciplinary divisions became more defined, a traditional A–F grading system was instituted, and the foreign language requirement was decreased. Faculty meetings became more technical and less exploratory; "many of the things had been discussed out," remembers theatre professor Carlson.

At the same time, faculty also tried wholly new approaches to higher education. Ashby Johnson, Tom West, and a few others created a separate curricular track, called "Jefferson House," for a select group of "mature" students to pursue whatever interested them without regard to requirements. West says they discontinued Jefferson House after a few years because students were having trouble getting into graduate school without certain required classes. "But it was fun," says West, "to take a student and say, 'What do you want to do with your life? What kinds of educational experiences would be of help to you? You can design some courses, you can develop independent studies, you can take the classes you want, and bring that all together and make it into a major.'" The college still allows students to create their own majors, but they have to meet a set of requirements as well.

Wireman encouraged a significant curricular and departmental overhaul in the early 1970s that became known as "Project '73." Months of serious inquiry and multiple working papers by faculty resulted in a variety of changes, some of which were soon abandoned, some of which exist to this day. For example, the college tried out a modular schedule of two-month-long classes that met every day; that experiment did not last. A three-week "autumn term" orientation for freshmen still exists to expose new students to college life and new learning strategies before the upperclassmen arrive on campus.

Western Civilization and Its Christian Heritage was redefined as new faculty brought their own reading suggestions, themes, and priorities. The course was shortened from two years to one and included more contemporary readings and attention to a wider diversity of ideas and influences. For much of the 1970s, the Core course was called "Inquiry and Human Nature" in the first semester of the freshman year and "Values and the Search for Spirit" in the second semester. According to longtime Eckerd College dean of faculty Lloyd W. Chapin, the revisions in the core curriculum "clearly treated Christianity more and more as simply one intellectual option among others." Interdisciplinary study, small seminar classes, and a focus on informed value judgments remained important, but "a core curriculum based on common content had been replaced by an emphasis on the diversity of human ways of knowing and choosing."[107] In 1980 the freshman Core course was once again renamed as "Western Heritage" with a renewed emphasis on classic Western texts; it is now called "Western Heritage in a Global Context."

A significant result of Project '73 was the organizing of faculty and disciplines into "collegia" that were meant to demonstrate the interrelatedness of knowledge and bring together academic areas that shared a similar approach to learning. The college is still organized into the Behavioral Sciences, Comparative Cultures, Creative Arts, Letters, and Natural Sciences and Mathematics collegia. The role of chairperson for each collegium rotates among the faculty in that group.

Jim Crane was chairman of the Creative Arts Collegium (CRA) one year when the administration asked each chair to develop objectives for his or her group. Never one to take committee responsibilities too seriously, Crane based his objectives on the ten commandments: "I said, 'CRA aims to reduce killing by ninety percent. We will reduce the coveting of other faculty wives by fifty percent.' And so on."

During this same period Wireman also spearheaded an official change in relationship between the college and the Presbyterian Church. In June 1971 the two Presbyterian synods transferred full control of the college to a self-perpetuating board of trustees and changed their role from owners of the college to a "covenant relationship" between the college and the church.

Late one night soon after Billy Wireman became president, athletic director Jim Harley heard a knock on his door. It was Billy, Jim's boss and one of his oldest friends. He told Jim he had been at a meeting with drugstore magnate Jack Eckerd, and now he was tired and needed a drink and a friend's company.

Money to keep the college going had become a paramount concern for Wireman and the FPC board. The 1970s were a tough time for liberal arts colleges all over the country as the national economy dipped, student enrollments in colleges dropped, increasingly prevalent community colleges offered the basics for much less tuition, the value of liberal arts learning was superseded by an emphasis on job preparation, an overall trend favoring public instead of private postsecondary enrollment picked up speed, and donor support wavered in the wake of student unrest. Jack Eckerd was a trustee with the college when

Wireman became president, and he was one of Wireman's first and best options for a large financial gift. But it would take years of nurturing to see it through.

"I know how hard he was working," says Harley of President Wireman. "We've had some powerful people almost brought to their knees by that job. It's just that demanding. We tried to do too much for too many people for too long. We got great results, but it's such a struggle financially to make it happen."

Sarah Dean remembers, "There were crises for the institution, crises for the students, crises for me, crises in our planning for the future, and, of course, financial crises just galore. We really did think that at one point we were going to go under. We thought we would merge with the University of South Florida or merge with New College in Sarasota. It was just one crisis after another. But, in the midst of that crisis, there was this wonderful tension that brought out the very best. . . . There was this vision that they had on the executive staff that seemed to just lift us and carry us through these crises that we had."

Jim Crane was feeling the financial worries of the college particularly keenly one afternoon, so he asked a friend to take a walk with him. Crane was despondent, he told his friend, over financial problems that had caused *Motive* magazine—the highly regarded Methodist publication to which he had submitted cartoons over the years—to fold. And now it looked as if the college where he had created such an innovative art program for undergraduates might also go under. But he remembers his friend saying, "You know, the real college is what happened between you and your students and you and your colleagues. And even if the college folds, that will go on and on and on."

The comment lifted Crane's spirits. He realized that "the thing that is of most lasting importance is the relationship between people. I see it like somebody sparked me, and I sparked my students, and they sparked somebody else, and maybe we can get enough sparks going to bring some light to this miserable dark world."

Fortunately, Crane and the rest of the faculty and students were able to keep that cycle of sparks going when Jack Eckerd came through with a ten million dollar gift to FPC in 1971. A small businessman with big ideas in the 1950s, Eckerd had bought three money-losing drugstores in Florida and had since built his company into an empire. Although not deeply religious at the time he joined FPC's board, and rather exasperated by some of the radical behaviors of students and faculty, he also respected risk taking. Wireman knew Jack Eckerd was passionate about trying "new and interesting" things and was attracted to quality people like those he found at FPC. He would often say to Wireman, "Billy, you guys are crazy down there and I don't understand what you're doing, but, boy, those kids are bright. And they're our future."

Wireman was vacationing in Blowing Rock, North Carolina, in May 1971, when Jack Eckerd called him one morning. He said, "Billy, I've read your proposal, and I'm probably not going to do it, it's a crazy idea, but when you get a minute, stop by." Wireman, who had a pilot's license and a small plane, immediately flew back to St. Petersburg. He saw Eckerd the next morning, and Jack agreed to give the ten million dollars.

Wireman says it was his own idea to rename Florida Presbyterian College to Eckerd College in recognition of Jack's generous decision. Changing the name of the college was not a condition of the gift. Board members claimed that the original name of the college was always considered temporary, and they were finding that the sectarian word *Presbyterian* was making it difficult to garner some grants. Eckerd himself resisted the idea, while Wireman wooed him with reminders of the Vanderbilts, Stanfords, and Dukes. Jack eventually relented, and Florida Presbyterian College officially changed its name to Eckerd College on July 1, 1972.

Many faculty and students were unhappy with the decision. Ken Keeton felt the college had made its reputation nationally as Florida Presbyterian and would now have to start all over. Students printed T-shirts and painted signs on the highway pointing visitors to "Eckerd 'Drug' College." On the other hand, Ashby Johnson felt that "Florida Presbyterian" was in some ways a handicap by suggesting the college had only a regional reach and was a sectarian institution, neither of which was the case.

The name change proved not to be fatal, and the infusion of cash may have saved the college's life, although financial challenges remained serious for many more years. Over time Eckerd College earned its own national recognition, as faculty, students, and administrators continued to pursue a vision of a liberal arts college of high quality and innovation emphasizing close student-teacher relationships, core learning experiences, independent study, and a lively encounter with religious faith.

US News & World Report named Eckerd one of the five most innovative colleges in America in 1987. In the 1990s Eckerd ranked twenty-fourth among over three thousand colleges in the nation in the percentage of graduates who attained PhD degrees.

In December 2002 the Policy Center on the First Year of College (funded by the Pew Charitable Trusts and the Atlantic Philanthropies) selected Eckerd College as one of the nation's top thirteen "Institutions of Excellence in the First College Year." In a study reported in a 2003 article in the *Chronicle of Higher Education*, Eckerd was the top-ranked college in America in the percentage of students who study abroad. In February 2004, the college installed its Phi Beta Kappa chapter, placing it among the youngest of the nation's 270 colleges and universities granted Phi Beta Kappa chapters.

The college continues to ask, "What is the right thing to do?" and "How can we do it?" It has reached out to nonresidential, adult students who are seeking a college degree after years in the workforce through its "Program for Experienced Learners" (PEL). Offering college courses, taught by Eckerd faculty, in six locations throughout Tampa Bay, PEL has graduated over four thousand students, most of whom have continued to work while studying.

Eckerd has brought the wealth of knowledge of distinguished retirees to its students and brought intellectual rigor to the later years of life through its "Academy of Senior Professionals at Eckerd College" (ASPEC). Over 300 members, including Elie Wiesel and the late James Michener, have been selected to join ASPEC on the basis of successful careers in business, academics, government, and the arts. ASPEC encourages intergenerational learning by connecting members with faculty and students. Members also organize and participate in educational seminars, lecture series, and performances on the college campus.

Eckerd has sustained Jack Bevan's commitment to seeking the most promising ideas in higher education while taking advantage of the unique resources of this particular community through such efforts as service-learning activities in St. Petersburg, greater attention to women's studies, expanded international experiences, a better understanding of environmental responsibility, and an appreciation of the educational value of the college's own waterfront (with such programs as a marine sciences major and a nationally known search-and-rescue boat service called EC-SAR). Says former dean of students Sarah Dean, "We're constantly revamping and revising our curriculum and our life at Eckerd so that we can address the issues of the day. It's a contemporary kind of place. It's not a place that just sort of gets stuck and comfortable."

At the same time, Eckerd College seeks to stay grounded in its most fundamental values. While it responds to current demands for an education that is relevant to career preparation, for example, it also remains loyal to, as Wireman put it, "the concept of the liberal arts being a seedbed from which you can make not only a living but a life."

Students who come to Eckerd College still see it as somehow different from other colleges, still a little risky, a little off the wall. They value it as a community where innovation and independence outweigh tradition and reputation. They recognize that this college calls to the best in them, offers much support and guidance, will do whatever it takes to create an individualized learning experience, and then expects the student to make the most of it.

In an address to the parents of students entering the college in 1967, President Bill Kadel talked about Moses leading the people of Israel out of Egypt. He reminded the crowd that,

"In the midst of frustration, futility and complaints that it couldn't be done, Moses said to the people of Israel, 'Stand still and see the salvation of God.' The trouble with us is that we don't stand still enough. We become so busy doing the things we have to do that we don't realize that it isn't entirely our problem and it doesn't all depend on our resources. This college will succeed because we are right, if we are right, and I think and pray we are."[108]

Eckerd College has never ceased exploring the relationship between the college and the church, between higher education and religious teachings, between the life of the mind and the life of the spirit. The results have never been particularly clear, but the important questions continue to be asked in a context of acceptance, moral responsibility, character, forgiveness, humor, and love. It's what the founders had envisioned. Time has proven them right.

Epilogue

Whoever touched that institution at that particular point as a member of the founding faculty or early faculty has certainly left a little bit of their soul there, and I can say without any reservation that a little bit of my soul remained and still remains at FPC and now Eckerd.

Billy Wireman

Billy Wireman left the presidency of Eckerd College in 1977, older and wiser, still concerned about the college's financial health but with every right to be proud of his accomplishments there. He continued an illustrious career in educational leadership, including the presidency of Queens College (now Queens University) in Charlotte, North Carolina (where Hunter Blakely had also been president). Wireman retired from Queens in 2002.

When he left Eckerd College, Wireman was succeeded by Peter Armacost, who served the college until 2000, during which time enrollment grew to over fifteen hundred residential students and twelve hundred non-residential students in the Program for Experienced Learners. Armacost was succeeded by Eckerd's current president, Donald R. Eastman III.

Many of the founding faculty stayed at Eckerd for the rest of their careers. Clark Bouwman, Ashby Johnson, George Reid, and Bill Wilbur all retired in the mid-1980s. Jim Crane, Iggy Foster, Keith Irwin, Bob Meacham, and Pedro Trakas also finished their careers at Eckerd and continued to be involved in teaching or other programs there.

Peter Meinke remained at Eckerd until his retirement in 1993. Like the children of Meacham, Keeton, West, and many others, all of Meinke's children attended Eckerd College. They went on to graduate school (three have Ph.D. degrees, one has an M.A. in art) and have pursued impressive careers.

Over the years Ken Keeton had offers to go elsewhere but says, "Nothing ever came up to the level of Eckerd. . . . I just never found anything like this at all." He stayed until his retirement in 1995.

Jim Harley occasionally considered moving on to a bigger athletic program somewhere else, but nothing captured his heart like the community at Eckerd. He retired from the college in 2002 but almost immediately returned as executive director of athletics advancement.

Tom West officially retired in 1994, but he still has an office at Eckerd College that he comes to every day. He works with students of all ages in various courses and programs, and he still has the same warm sparkle in his eyes that convinced those first freshmen to take a leap of faith and join him at a brand-new college. West recently told founding freshman and board trustee Grover Wrenn, "I just think the day I get up and don't feel like I want to teach a class is the day I'll die."

Parabasis

In his legendary lecture, "Myth and Symbol," which he gave several times in the early years of Florida Presbyterian College, founding faculty member John Satterfield ends with a parabasis. In ancient Greek comedy, he explains, an author could include a section in which the chorus would speak about things the author deemed important to himself. I conclude this book with my own such aside, so that readers may know something of my motivation, biases, qualifications, and passion for the story of the college's beginning.

I can't remember when I didn't know of FPC / Eckerd College. The founding president, Bill Kadel, had already been gone from the college a year before I was born in St. Petersburg in 1969. But he had moved on to the presidency of Pittsburgh Theological Seminary, which was only a three-hour drive from the West Virginia mountains where I grew up. So I visited my grandfather often in his home there, traveling with my parents, Richard and Karen Kadel, who had met at FPC as founding freshmen.

My father, Dick, had graduated from Boone High in Orlando and then served three years in the marines. He came back to Florida just in time for the opening of FPC, where he joined the choir, one of the best organized extracurricular opportunities in that first year. My mother, Karen Reynolds, was a graduate of St. Petersburg High; her parents directed the music program at Christ United Methodist Church in downtown St. Pete. Both my parents came to FPC that first year because they were offered financial aid. Both claim they didn't feel like the serious, top-notch students others were in that first freshman class.

They met in the choir and even performed an operetta together for a winter term project. By the end of their sophomore year they were married. They didn't graduate from FPC, because my father wanted a teaching certificate so he could pursue a career in music with the stability of a teaching job. Since FPC didn't yet offer that option, he transferred to Florida State University in Tallahassee. My mother left school to work to support my dad.

In 1974 my parents and their four kids moved to Elkins, West Virginia, where my father headed up the music program at a small Presbyterian liberal arts college called Davis & Elkins College. My mother finished her degree there. I got the best public school education an isolated town of eight thousand people could provide.

Whenever we visited my Kadel grandparents, I was aware that my grandfather was a highly respected professional, and I could tell that my father revered him. But Bill Kadel was not unapproachable as a grandfather. He took us to pick blackberries, let us ride his lawn mower, and taught us to play card games with penny bets. He always asked me what I was up to in my life, and as I grew, I began to listen to him hold forth at the dinner table about politics and social welfare. I realized I wanted to please this great man, to impress him with my own life choices.

I am told that my older brother and sister visited our grandparents at Lewis House—the president's home on the FPC campus in the late 1960s. I don't remember setting foot on the campus of what I knew as Eckerd College until I came to school there as a freshman in 1985, the same year my parents moved back to St. Petersburg. I first enrolled at Eckerd because the school provided financial help. I was sixteen, I lived three miles from campus at home with my parents, and I thought I wanted to become a teacher like my dad.

Eckerd College suited me perfectly—or perhaps I was molded so that I suited it. Either way, it was a great match. My experience of student life was limited since I lived off-campus, but I craved intellectual challenge, and Eckerd provided it. With excellent professors in Western Heritage, psychology, anthropology, poetry, and education, I became curious about fields of study I'd never even thought of before. I became part of an honors program and a Ford Foundation–sponsored interdisciplinary program. I hung on every word at talks given by Jimmy Carter, Allen Ginsberg, Maxine Greene, and Alex Haley. I spent a semester in London. I pursued independent studies in science and sociology. I worked in the library, sang in the choir, and often went barefoot to class. And when it came time to be a student teacher at the local elementary school, I went to my mentor, Kathy Watson, in tears because I had discovered I no longer wanted to be a teacher.

"I was just waiting for you to figure that out," Kathy said to me. She wasn't a bit worried that I only had one year before graduation and wanted to change my major. In what I came to think of as typical Eckerd style, we devised a "concentration" of my very own: "Education and Qualitative Research." I learned to do participant observation in classrooms and conduct interviews with teachers and students, and I wrote a senior thesis about a private, alternative school in St. Pete.

At graduation in 1989 I was honored with the Philip J. Lee Honor Award for "academic achievement and future promise." A weighty award for a twenty-year-old it seems to me now but more meaningful with my better understanding of who Philip Lee, FPC's first board chairman, was. That same year Kathy Watson received the Robert A. Staub Distinguished Professor of the Year Award. And my grandfather, Bill Kadel, gave the commencement address and hugged me on the stage when I came up for my diploma. (I made sure to zip up my red "Creative Arts Collegium" robe to hide the cut-off jean shorts and T-shirt that seemed appropriate garb for an Eckerd graduation.) It was one of the most satisfying days of my life. I hope it was for my mentor and for my grandfather, too.

From such a tangle of personal tales comes my desire to learn more about the founding of the college, to honor its past and the people who worked so hard and dreamed so big, and to do what I can to contribute to its future.

I imagine many small colleges end up choosing one of their own to write their history. But lest my involvement appear wholly nepotistic, I offer this brief list of qualifications. I went on to earn a master's degree at the University of Michigan and a Ph.D. degree in "cultural foundations of education" from Syracuse University, where I focused much of my study on the role of schooling in society, the history of higher education, and advanced qualitative methods. I worked as a researcher for the National Center on Postsecondary Teaching and Learning, and I taught undergraduates. Since then, I have worked as a professional writer in the fields of education and nonprofit management, and in 2000 I started my own business, TimePieces Personal Biographies, using my skill as an interviewer to write life histories and institutional histories based on people's stories.

A Note on Methodology

This is a book of stories about Florida Presbyterian / Eckerd College. Much can be gleaned from these stories about the purpose of higher education, the historical context in which the college was founded, the role of the church in a learning institution, the changing philosophy of the college, and the ongoing challenges of providing a liberal arts education in today's society. I hope you will discover some of that as you read.

But this book is not an analytical study seeking to draw such conclusions. It is a story of a dream made real. I wrote it to document the past before all the storytellers had left us.

While I used documents from the college's archives (newspaper articles, college newsletters, some meeting minutes), this story is primarily an oral history, drawn from interviews I conducted in 2003 as well as recorded interviews from the 1970s through 1990s done by other students and faculty. The people I chose to interview were not a random or representative sample. I interviewed most of the founding faculty who were still alive. I also contacted a few founding faculty wives, some of the professors hired in the first few years after the founding, and an admittedly small number of students to fill in a bit of the student perspective.

Founding faculty member Ashby Johnson once said, "I'm not interested in history. I'm interested in mythology. Eckerd College (Florida Presbyterian College) has a historical reality. Its mythic reality is more important. Somehow I've always looked on history as the 'lies that the victors tell about the past'; mythology is the 'interesting lies that we tell about our past.' But it's true in the sense that it deals with the true feelings, and, hell, that's what I'm interested in."[109]

I tried to be accurate with as many of the facts and figures as I could verify. But I let the feelings and the mythic reality stand. I let the voices of the college community tell as much of the story as possible in their own words. I hope you are enlightened and entertained by this story. I hope you feel the same awe and gratitude I have felt while writing it.

Acknowledgments

The narrative of this book relies heavily on the stories told by its founders. So many people welcomed me into their homes and opened their minds and hearts to me (see Appendix B). For that, I am forever grateful. In addition to the interviews I conducted, much of the research I used has been accumulating over several decades as various people associated with FPC / Eckerd College have documented aspects of its history. I offer thanks to all my predecessors in this endeavor and especially to college archivist, Cathy McCoy, for helping me access previously recorded interviews, scrapbooks, official college publications, and other archival materials, and for answering specific queries with detailed and referenced responses.

Members of my family have also provided information and their own memories, including my parents, Richard and Karen Kadel, my aunt, Pinky Moore, and my late grandmother, Kay Kadel. My husband, Jeff Taras, fed my efforts with his own excitement about this project as he read countless sections and drafts. My assistant, Marti Murphy, coded hundreds of pages of data; Dawn Regan Ellenburg, the book's designer, and Elizabeth Gratch, the world's best copy editor, turned my work into art. President Don Eastman believed enough in the project and in me to make it possible.

Finally, my life and this book have been transformed by my mentor, Kathy Watson, now associate dean and assistant to the president of Eckerd College. Her guidance of this book from inception to completion and the joy of our collaboration have strengthened me and this story. Knowing that I thrive when loved, she has been unstinting. I am blessed.

Appendix A:
THE FOUNDING FACULTY

FOUNDING FACULTY OF FLORIDA PRESBYTERIAN COLLEGE

Dr. John M. Bevan, Dean of Faculty

Dr. Dennis E. Anderson, Instructor in Biology

Mr. Guy Owen Baker, Assistant Professor of Music

Dr. Clark Bouwman,
Associate Professor of Sociology

Dr. A. Howard Carter,
Chairman of Division of Humanities

Miss Bettye Rae Crane,
Instructor in Physical Education

Mr. Joe B. Davis, Laboratory Assistant in Chemistry

Dr. John W. Dixon, Associate Professor of Art

Dr. Everett Emerson, Associate Professor of English

Dr. I. G. Foster, Chairman of Division
of Math & Natural Sciences

Mr. Robert Hall, Instructor in French

Mr. William Fletcher Harrison, Jr.,
Cataloger, Instructor / Librarian

Dr. E. Ashby Johnson,
Professor of Religion & Philosophy

FOUNDING FACULTY OF FLORIDA PRESBYTERIAN COLLEGE
(CONTINUED)

DR. KENNETH E. KEETON,
ASSISTANT PROFESSOR OF GERMAN

DR. ROBERT MEACHAM, PROFESSOR OF MATHEMATICS

MR. CREIGHTON PEDEN, CHAPLAIN ASSISTANT
(UNIVERSITY OF CHICAGO THEOLOGICAL SEMINARY)

DR. GEORGE K. REID, PROFESSOR OF BIOLOGY

MR. JOHN SATTERFIELD, ASSOCIATE PROFESSOR OF MUSIC

MISS FLORENCE SHERBOURNE, ASSISTANT PROFESSOR,
DEVELOPMENTAL ENGLISH & READING

MR. STEWART P. SMITH, CHIEF LIBRARIAN

DR. DEXTER SQUIBB, ASSISTANT PROFESSOR OF CHEMISTRY

DR. PEDRO TRAKAS, PROFESSOR OF SPANISH

DR. J. THOMAS WEST, DIRECTOR OF ADMISSIONS

MRS. FRANCES WHITAKER, DEAN OF WOMEN

DR. FREDERIC R. WHITE, PROFESSOR OF CLASSICS

DR. WILLIAM C. WILBUR,
ASSOCIATE PROFESSOR OF HISTORY

DR. JACK C. WILSON,
ASSISTANT PROFESSOR OF MATHEMATICS

MR. BILLY O. WIREMAN,
ASSISTANT PROFESSOR OF PHYSICAL EDUCATION

Source: Florida Presbyterian College Newsletter (1960, April)

Appendix B:
INTERVIEWEES

The following people were interviewed by the author in the process of researching this history. All but two were interviewed in person, either in their homes or Eckerd College offices. Horton and Bevan were interviewed over the telephone.

LOUISE BEVAN
CLARK BOUWMAN
JIM CARLSON
MARJORIE CARTER
JIM CRANE
SARAH DEAN
CAROLYN HALL HORTON
JIM HARLEY
KEITH IRWIN
KENNETH KEETON
KATHARINE MEACHAM
PETER MEINKE
JOHN SATTERFIELD
STERLING WATSON
TOM WEST
WILLIAM C. WILBUR
BILLY O. WIREMAN
GROVER WRENN

Notes

Chapter 1

1   Wilbur, W. C. (1994, April 18). Prolegomena to a history of FPC/Eckerd College. Address at the Amateurs Dinner, President's Dining Room, Eckerd College, St. Petersburg, Florida.

2   All quotations not attributed to a particular source by way of an endnote are excerpted from the recorded interviews I conducted in 2003. These interviews were transcribed verbatim. When inserting a quotation into the text, I occasionally made slight edits to the verbatim statement to improve the flow of the words. These edits did not reorder words, remove significant amounts of text (unless indicated by an ellipsis), or change the meaning of a statement in any way. They correct for the halting nature of speech, or occasionally change the tense of a statement, to allow for easier reading.

3   A portrait of Jack Bevan that captures his intensity now hangs in the faculty lounge—named the Bevan Lounge—in the Hough Center on the campus of Eckerd College.

4   Wilbur, W. C. (1989, June). Interview of John Bevan.

5   Wilbur, W. C. (1989, June). Interview of John Bevan.

Chapter 2

6   Johnke, P. (1974). Telephone interview of William H. Kadel.

7   Wilbur, W. C. (1989, June). Interview of John Bevan.

8   Wilbur, W. C. (1994, April 18). Prolegomena to a history of FPC/Eckerd College. Address at the Amateurs Dinner, President's Dining Room, Eckerd College, St. Petersburg, Florida.

9   Johnke, P. (1974, April). Telephone interview of John Bevan.

10   Johnke, P. (1974, April). Telephone interview of John Bevan.

11   Johnke, P. (1974, April). Telephone interview of John Bevan.

12   Meacham Keane, L. (2002, February). Memorial service: Reflections on the professional life of Robert C. Meacham, Ph.D. Griffin Chapel, Eckerd College, St. Petersburg, Florida.

13   Johnson, E. A. (1976, January 11). Interview of John Satterfield.

14   Johnke, P. (1974, April). Telephone interview of John Bevan.

15   Zimnik, M. (1987, May 21). *Crosses and Crises, 1960-1987: Twenty-seven years of Florida Presbyterian and Eckerd College. The Triton Tribune* (Special 20th Edition Archive Issue), p. 29.

16   Johnson, E. A. (1974). *Reflections about the founding of Eckerd College.* Unpublished manuscript.

17   Johnke, P. (1974, April). Telephone interview of John Bevan.

Chapter 3

18   Brandle, L. (1958, September 16). Dr. William H. Kadel – new university president. *St. Petersburg Times.*

19   Many of the statistics and details about FPC's start-up process in this and the next chapter come from W. C. Wilbur's "Prolegomena to a History of FPC/Eckerd College," an address delivered at the Amateurs Dinner in the President's Dining Room on April 18, 1994, at Eckerd College, St. Petersburg, Florida.

20   Johnke, P. (1974). Telephone interview of William H. Kadel.

21   Johnke, P. (1974). Telephone interview of William H. Kadel.

22   *Bulletin of Florida Presbyterian College: 1961-62, Vol. 2* (9).

23   Johnson, E. A. (1976, March 31). Interview of Alvin Eurich.

24   Brandle, L. (1958, September 16). Dr. William H. Kadel – new university president. *St. Petersburg Times.*

25   Brandle, L. (1958, September 16). Dr. William H. Kadel – new university president. *St. Petersburg Times.*

26   Brandle, L. (1958, September 16). Dr. William H. Kadel – new university president. *St. Petersburg Times.*

27   Kadel, W. H. (1990, March 19). Taped reminiscences.

28   Brandle, L. (1958, September 17). Dr. Kadel sets the goals for Presbyterian college. *St. Petersburg Times.*

Chapter 4

29   Doubleday, D. (1958, September 16). St. Petersburg site is chosen for Presbyterian university. *St. Petersburg Times.*

30   Johnson, T. C. (1894). *History of the Southern Presbyterian Church.* Digitized and published on-line by the Presbyterian Church of America Historical Center, St. Louis, Missouri, www.pcanet.org.

31   Winter, R. M. (2000). Division & reunion in the Presbyterian Church, U.S.: A Mississippi retrospective. *Journal of Presbyterian History, 78* (1).

32   Doubleday, D. (1958, September 16). St. Petersburg site is chosen for Presbyterian university. *St. Petersburg Times.*

33   Johnson, E. A. (1976, February 16). Interview of Philip Lee.

34   Stublen, N. (1959, April 10). College fund goes past $1.2 million. *St. Petersburg Evening Independent.*

35   Johnson, E. A. (1976, February 16). Interview of Philip Lee.

36   Minutes of the Joint Meeting of the Officers of the Board of Trustees of Florida Presbyterian College and the Officers of the Board of Trustees of the United Presbyterian College of Florida. (1958, September 15). Tampa, Florida.

37   Johnke, P. (1974). Telephone interview of William H. Kadel.

Chapter 5

38   *Report of Florida Presbyterian College to the Sixty-Ninth Annual Meeting, Synod of Florida, Presbyterian Church in the United States.* (1960, May 17-19). Tampa, Florida.

39   Wilbur, W. C. (1989, June). Interview of John Bevan.

40   Johnson, E. A. (1974). *Reflections about the founding of Eckerd College.* Unpublished manuscript.

41   Johnson, E. A. (1976, January 11). Interview of John Satterfield.

Chapter 6

42   From title page of college promotional handbook, the *Bulletin of Florida Presbyterian College: 1961-62, Vol. 2* (9).

43   Wilbur, W. C. (1989, June). Interview of John Bevan.

44 *Bulletin of Florida Presbyterian College: 1961-62, Vol. 2* (9).

45 Bevan, J. M. (1964). Florida Presbyterian College: New adventure in education. In W. H. Stickler (Ed.), *Experimental Colleges: Their Role in American Higher Education*. Tallahassee: Florida State University.

46 Johnke, P. (1974). Telephone interview of William H. Kadel

47 The substance of these early faculty meetings is re-created here using excerpts from memos written among the faculty in 1959 as they grappled with the plans for the "Western Civilization and Its Christian Heritage" course and using quotations excerpted from interviews conducted with individual faculty members many years later.

48 Satterfield, J. (1999, October 15). Unpublished remarks prior to the naming of the Eckerd College Faculty Lounge in honor of Dr. John Morgan Bevan and the founding faculty of Florida Presbyterian College. St. Petersburg, Florida.

49 Founding Faculty Reminiscence Meeting. (2002, June 9). St. Petersburg, Florida.

50 Johnson, E. A. (1976, January 11). Interview of John Satterfield.

51 *Bulletin of Florida Presbyterian College: 1961-62, Vol.2* (9).

52 Bevan, J. M. (1964). Florida Presbyterian College: New adventure in education. In W. H. Stickler (Ed.), *Experimental Colleges: Their Role in American Higher Education*. Tallahassee: Florida State University.

53 Johnson, E. A. (1976, January 11). Interview of John Satterfield.

54 Johnson, E. A. (1976, January 11). Interview of John Satterfield.

55 Wilbur, W. C. (1989, June). Interview of John Bevan.

Chapter 7

56 Kadel, W. H. (1960, September 16). Memo from the president. Florida Presbyterian College, St. Petersburg, Florida.

57 Kadel, W. H. (1960, May 20). Personal correspondence with Carolyn Ruth Hall. Florida Presbyterian College, St. Petersburg, Florida.

58 Kadel, W. H. (1990, March 19). Taped reminiscences.

59 Keeton, K. (1961). *Diary*.

60 Satterfield, J. (1999, October 15). Unpublished remarks prior to the naming of the Eckerd College Faculty Lounge in honor of Dr. John Morgan Bevan and the founding faculty of Florida Presbyterian College. St. Petersburg, Florida.

61   Satterfield, J. (1999, October 15). Unpublished remarks prior to the naming of the Eckerd College Faculty Lounge in honor of Dr. John Morgan Bevan and the founding faculty of Florida Presbyterian College. St. Petersburg, Florida.

62   Hoffman, P. E. (1964). An interpretive history of Florida Presbyterian College. *Yearbook: 1960-1964*. St. Petersburg: Florida Presbyterian College.

63   Faculty meeting minutes. (1960, December 16). Florida Presbyterian College, St. Petersburg, Florida.

64   Taped Reminiscences of Billy Wireman. (1990, March 7). Recorded in the president's office of Queens College, Charlotte, North Carolina.

65   We're Tritons! (1960, November). *Bulletin of Florida Presbyterian College, Vol. 2* (9), p. 3.

66   Meacham, K. (2000, March 1). The vision behind the founding of Eckerd College. Address as part of forum entitled "Transitions: Women—A Kaleidoscopic View," hosted by the Academy of Senior Professionals at Eckerd College. St. Petersburg, Florida.

67   Keeton, K. (1961). *Diary*.

68   Hoffman, P. E. (1964). An interpretive history of Florida Presbyterian College. *Yearbook: 1960-1964*. St. Petersburg: Florida Presbyterian College.

69   Hoffman, P. E. (1964). An interpretive history of Florida Presbyterian College. *Yearbook: 1960-1964*. St. Petersburg: Florida Presbyterian College.

Chapter 8

70   Founding Faculty Reminiscence Meeting. (1995, May 13). St. Petersburg, Florida.

71   Watson, V. S. (1993, May). Meinke's Retirement – or Goodbye to Blind Petey. Unpublished remarks delivered at Peter Meinke's retirement celebration. Eckerd College, St. Petersburg, Florida.

72   *Report of Florida Presbyterian College to the Sixty-Ninth Annual Meeting, Synod of Florida, Presbyterian Church in the United States.* (1960, May 17-19). Tampa, Florida.

73   Johnson, E. A. (1976, January 11). Interview of John Satterfield.

74   First ladies on campus. (1965). *St. Petersburg Times*.

75   Bevan, J. M.. Excerpts from "Betwixt and Between." Unpublished, undated paper.

76   Johnson, E. A. (1976, January 11). Interview of John Satterfield.

Chapter 9

77   Johnson, E. A. (1976, February 16). Interview of Philip Lee.

78   Wilbur, W. C. (1989, June). Interview of John Bevan.

79   Johnson, E. A. (1976, January 11). Interview of John Satterfield.

80   Satterfield, J. (1989, September). Taped reminiscences, recorded at his home.

81   Emerson, E.H., Secretary of the Faculty. (1962, May 25). Secretary's Report of Florida Presbyterian College faculty meeting, St. Petersburg, Florida.

82   Emerson, E.H., Secretary of the Faculty. (1962, May 31). Secretary's Report of Florida Presbyterian College faculty meeting, St. Petersburg, Florida.

83   Founding Faculty Reminiscence Meeting. (1995, May 13).

84   Sarratt, R. (1966). *The Ordeal of Desegregation: The First Decade*. New York: Harper & Row; Clark, R. P. & Arsenault, R., Eds. (2002). *The Changing South of Gene Patterson: Journalism and Civil Rights*, 1960-1968. Gainesville: University Press of Florida.

85   Johnke, P. (1974, April). Telephone interview of John Bevan.

86   Johnson, E. A. (1976, January 11). Interview of John Satterfield.

87   Johnson, E. A. (1976, January). Interview of Robert Sheen.

88   Keeton, K. (2002). *Gullible's Travels: An Autobiography*. St. Petersburg, Florida: Self-published.

89   College gets gift for Selma protest. (1965, March 23). *New York Times*, p. 28; No blackmail. (1965, March 23). *St. Petersburg Evening Independent.*

Chapter 10

90   Johnke, P. (1974). History of a dream. Unpublished manuscript. Eckerd College: St. Petersburg, Florida.

91   Johnson, E. A. (1976, February 16). Interview of Philip Lee.

92   Sheen, R. *His-Story*. (1991). St. Petersburg, Florida: Self-published.

93   Taped Reminiscences of Billy Wireman. (1990, March 7). Recorded in the president's office of Queens College, Charlotte, North Carolina.

94   Johnson, E. A. (1976, March 31). Interview of Alvin Eurich.

Chapter 11

95   Armacost, P. H. (1998). *Eckerd College: A Florida college of national distinction*. Address to the Newcomen Society of the United States.

96   Johnson, E. A. (1974). *Reflections about the founding of Eckerd College*. Unpublished manuscript.

97   Colleges: Coming of age at six. (1966, December 9). *Time Magazine*.

Chapter 12

98   Kadel, W. H. (1990, March 19). Taped reminiscences.

99   Taped Reminiscences of Billy Wireman. (1990, March 7). Recorded in the president's office of Queens College, Charlotte, North Carolina.

100   Kadel, W. H. (1967, May 1). Memo to the Trustees. Florida Presbyterian College, St. Petersburg.

101   Wilbur, W. C. (1989). Interview of John Bevan.

102   Kadel, W. H. (1968, May 17). A personal word to all our friends about my decision to leave Florida Presbyterian College. Letter from the Office of the President, St. Petersburg.

103   Kadel-Taras, S. (1998). *Taking Life As It Comes: The Life Story of Katharine Naylor Kadel*. Ann Arbor, Michigan: Self-published.

Chapter 13

104   Frasca, J. (1968). Nice guy runs a college. *Tampa Tribune*.

105   Moorhead, J. (1968, July 2). New chief, new era for college. *St. Petersburg Independent*.

106   West, T. (2002, February). Interview of Billy Wireman; Johnke, P. (1974, April). Interview of Billy Wireman.

107   Chapin, L. W. (2000). The core curriculum at Eckerd College. In M. Nelson & Associates (Eds.), *Alive at the Core: Exemplary Approaches to General Education in the Humanities* (pp. 96-122). San Francisco: Jossey-Bass.

108   Kadel, W. H. The parents' role in the future of Florida Presbyterian College. (1967, September 1). Unpublished address to the parents of entering students.

A Note on Methodology

109   Johnson, E. A. (1974). *Reflections about the founding of Eckerd College*. Unpublished manuscript.